Aesthetic Empathy

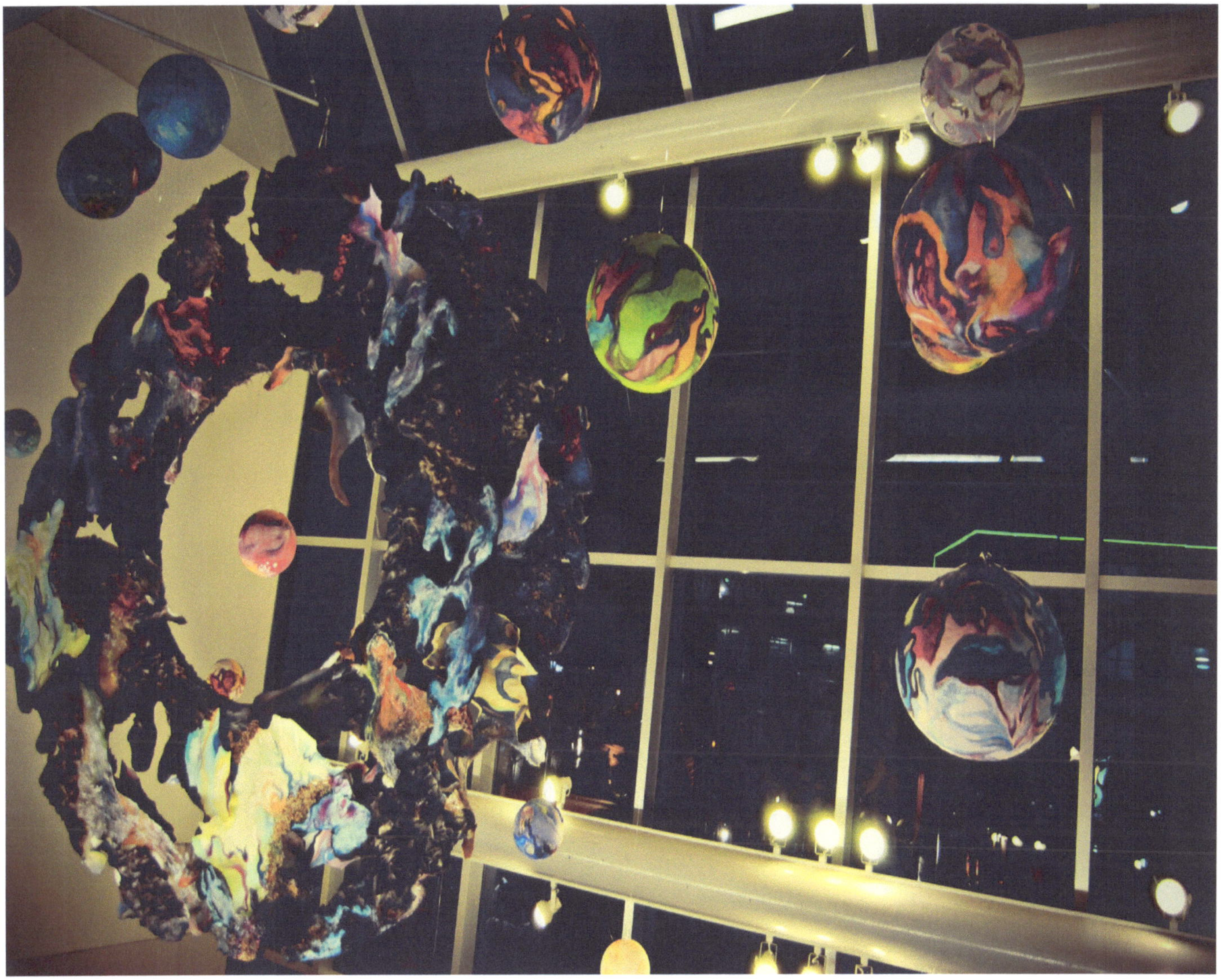

InSoon S. Felch

Artist Statement

I do not hesitate to translate my emotions through my art works, Painting as life's metaphor to interest me, which can be manifest either in shaped canvas or incorporated with sculptural forms. Introducing sculptural element to the work would transform not merely the appearance but the fundamental structure of shaped-canvas painting. I have explored the relief involving edges elaborated by a variety of medium and materials and a painterly attack. Through multiple layers, which create radical surfaces and add a new quality of three-dimensional forms, this new technique easily lands a sculptural element to the work.

Although primarily non-objective and non-representational, I consider my work an intensely subjective response to the various aspects of the painterly reality around me: lines, colors, figures, and shapes. These geometric shapes and calligraphic gestures, in the overall complex relationships with other figures and spatial element, play in a curiously ambiguous ways as counterpoints. I did not begin employing pre-determined symbols; rather, I have tried to neither abstract nor abstracted art. For there is a conscious artistic will and subjective selection of images: I begin with an "image," which I move and turn around until it is transformed into a form that departs far from the initial images. I leave the meaning and interpretation of the work to the free aesthetic choice of the viewer.

As a postscript I would like to say…that though I cannot over-emphasize the importance and influence of the Western art and aesthetics in shaping my artistic direction, nor can I deny or ignore the strong workings of my Eastern cultural root that inherently nurtured my aesthetic taste and inclination…all art forms being faithful mirrors of the cultural "landscapes".

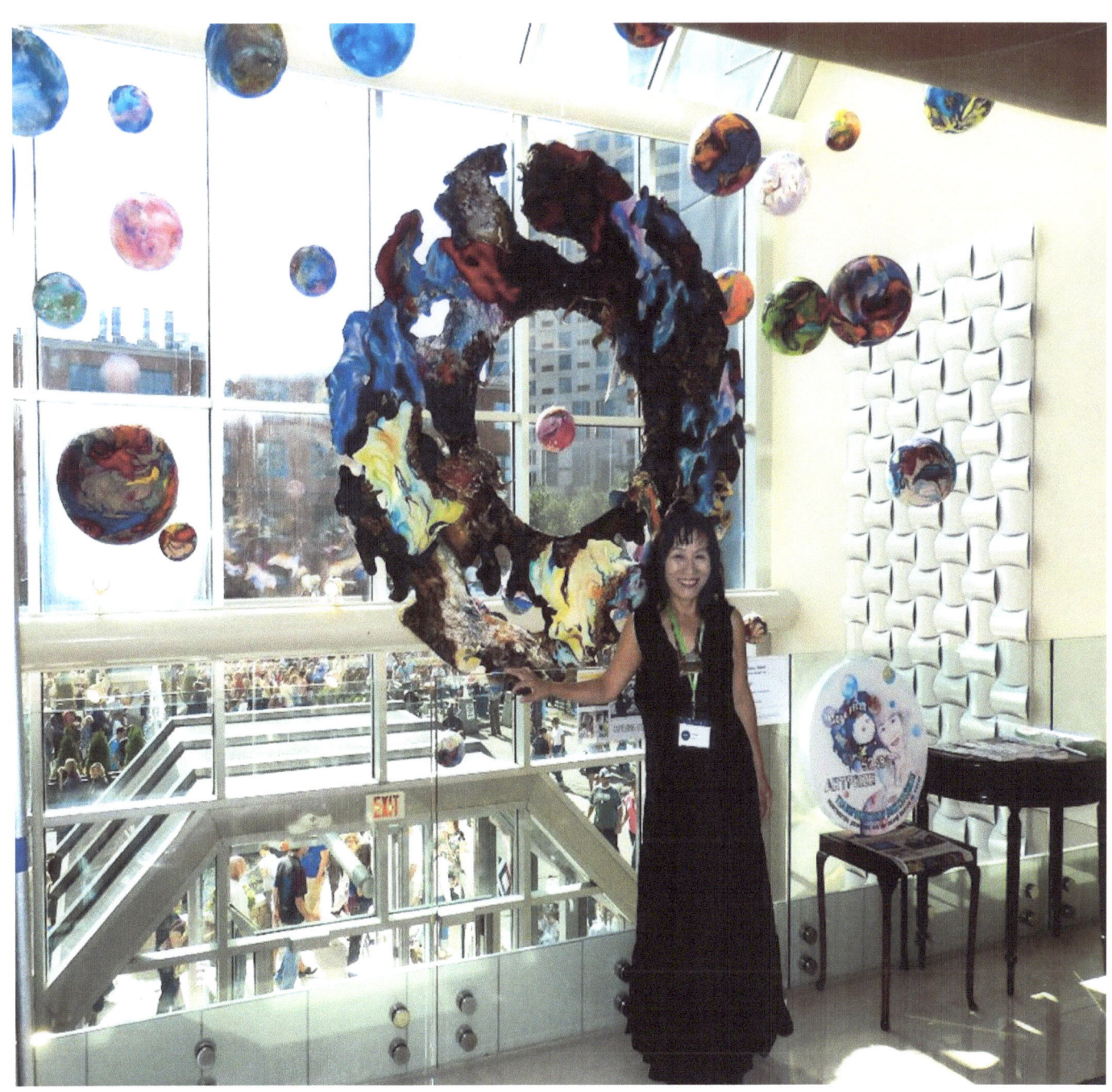

Transformation of Consciousness
Photo by Cathy Sorensen

ArtPrize 2012 International Art Competition, Grand Rapids, MI

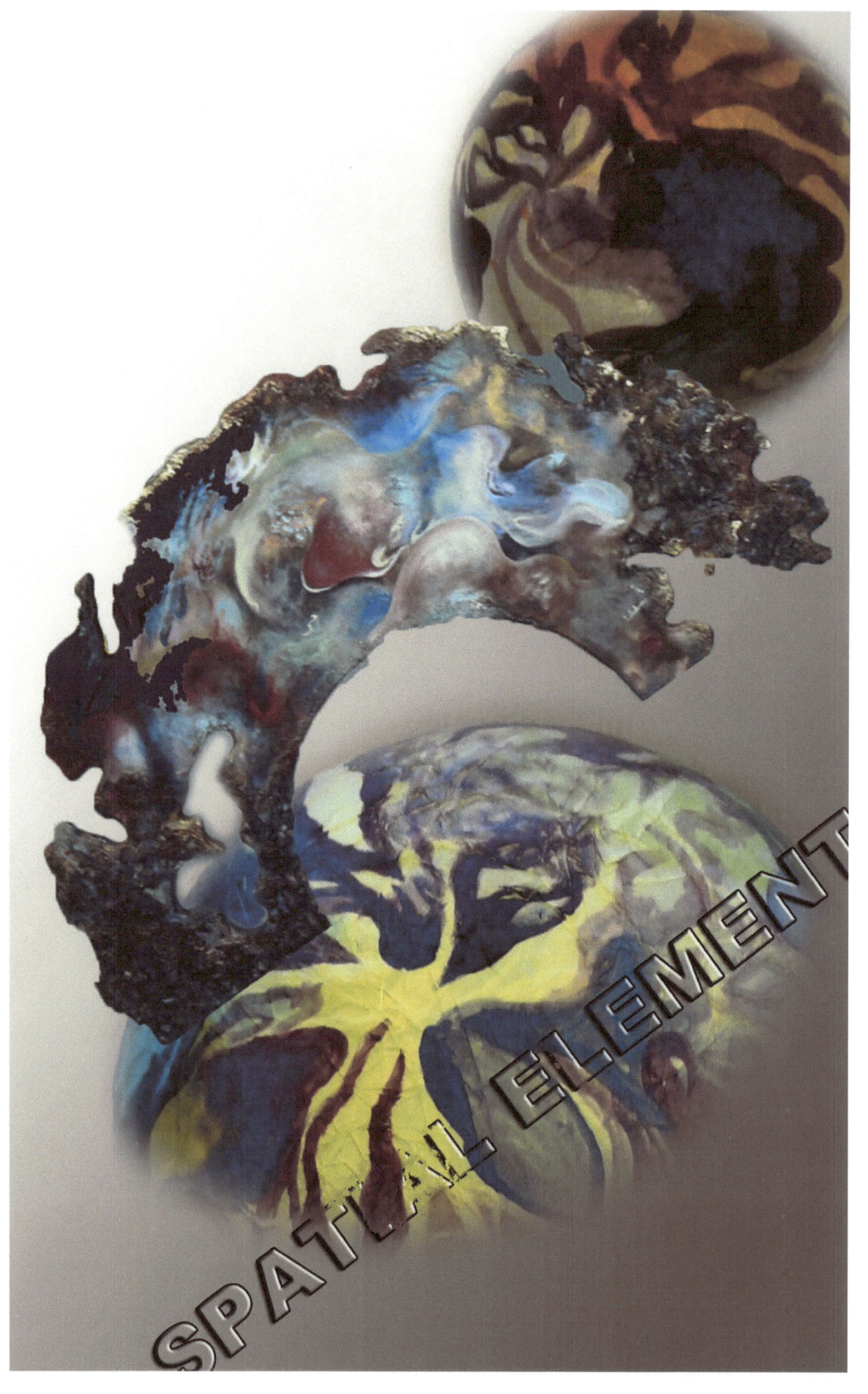

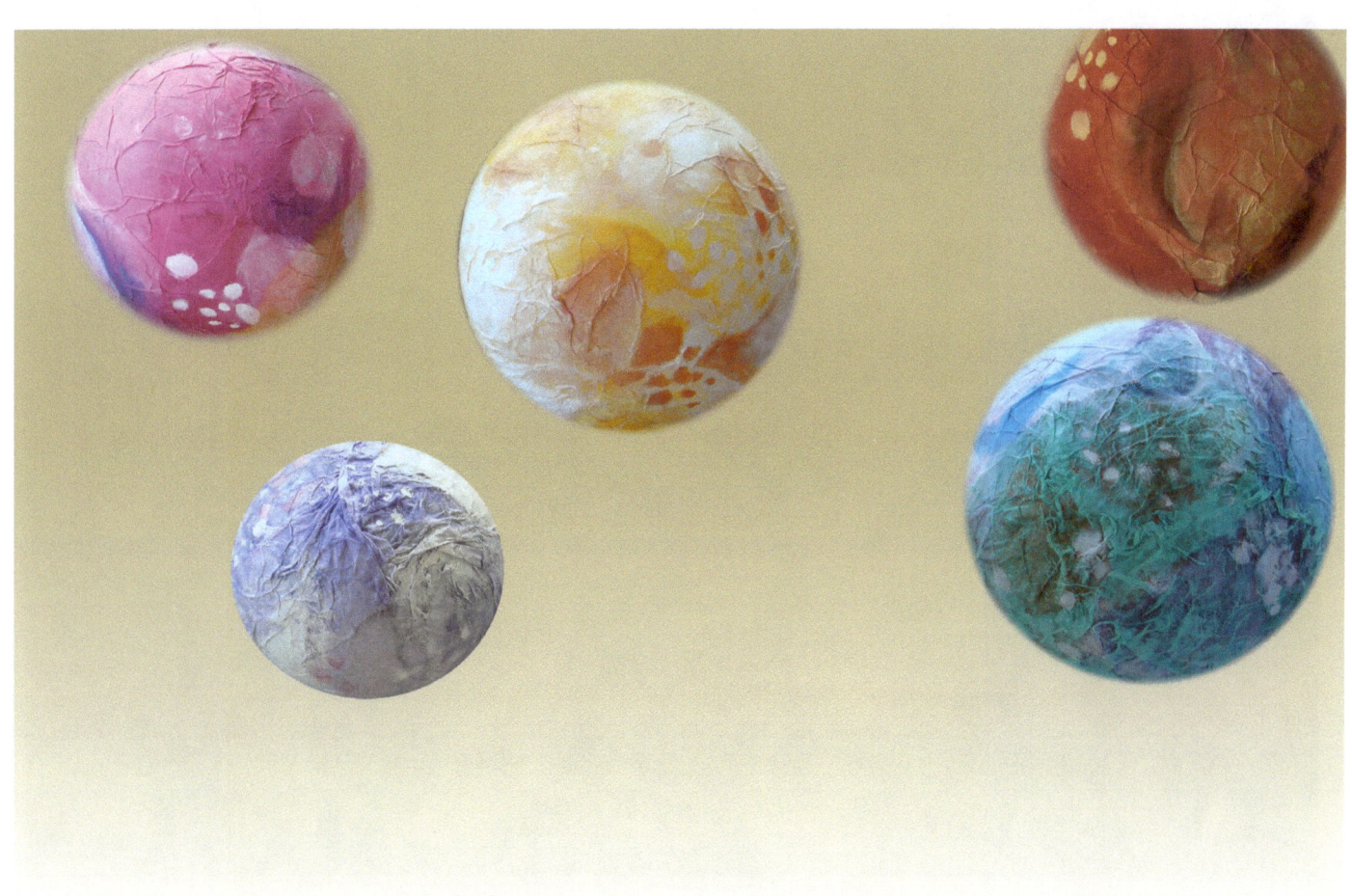

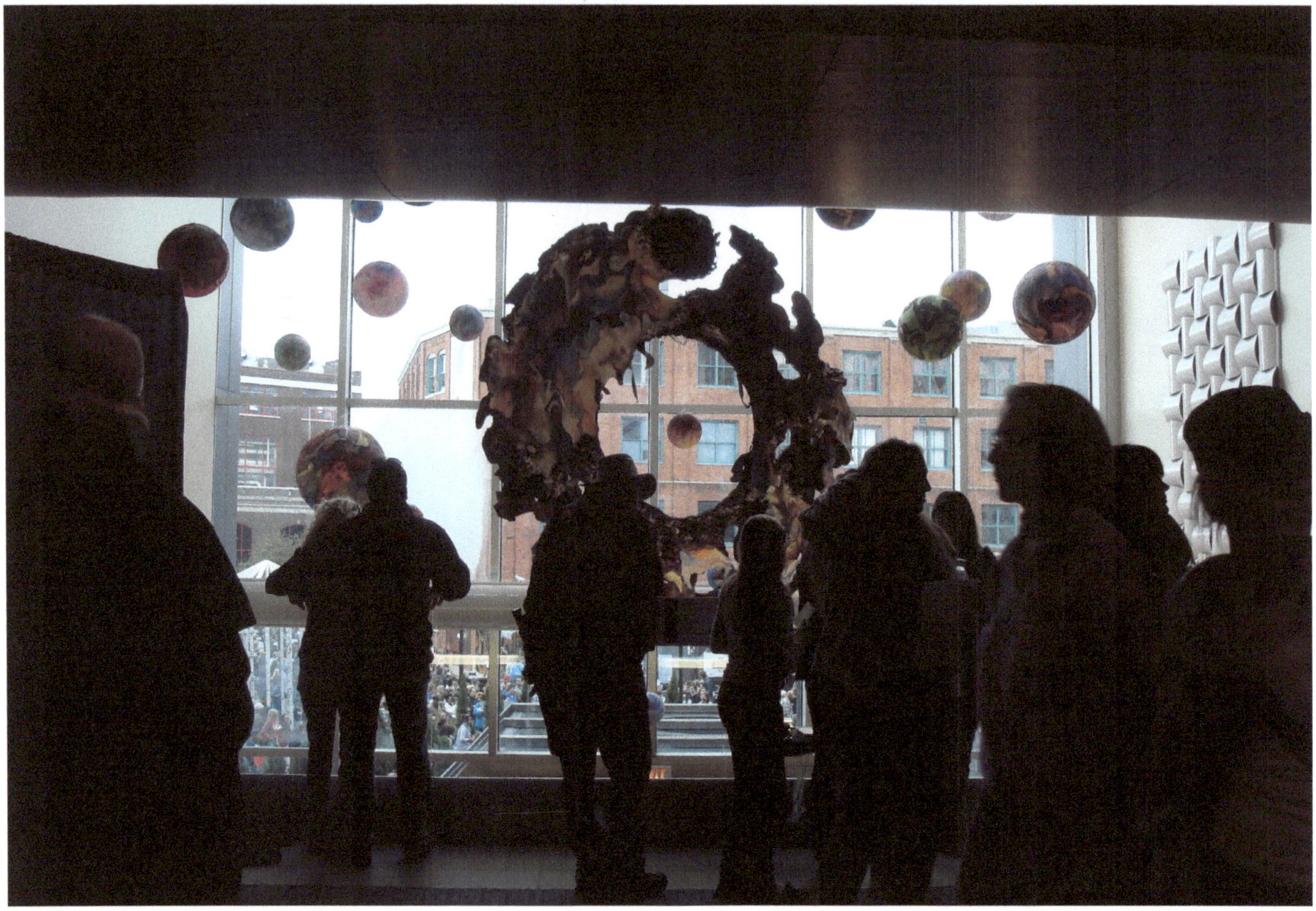

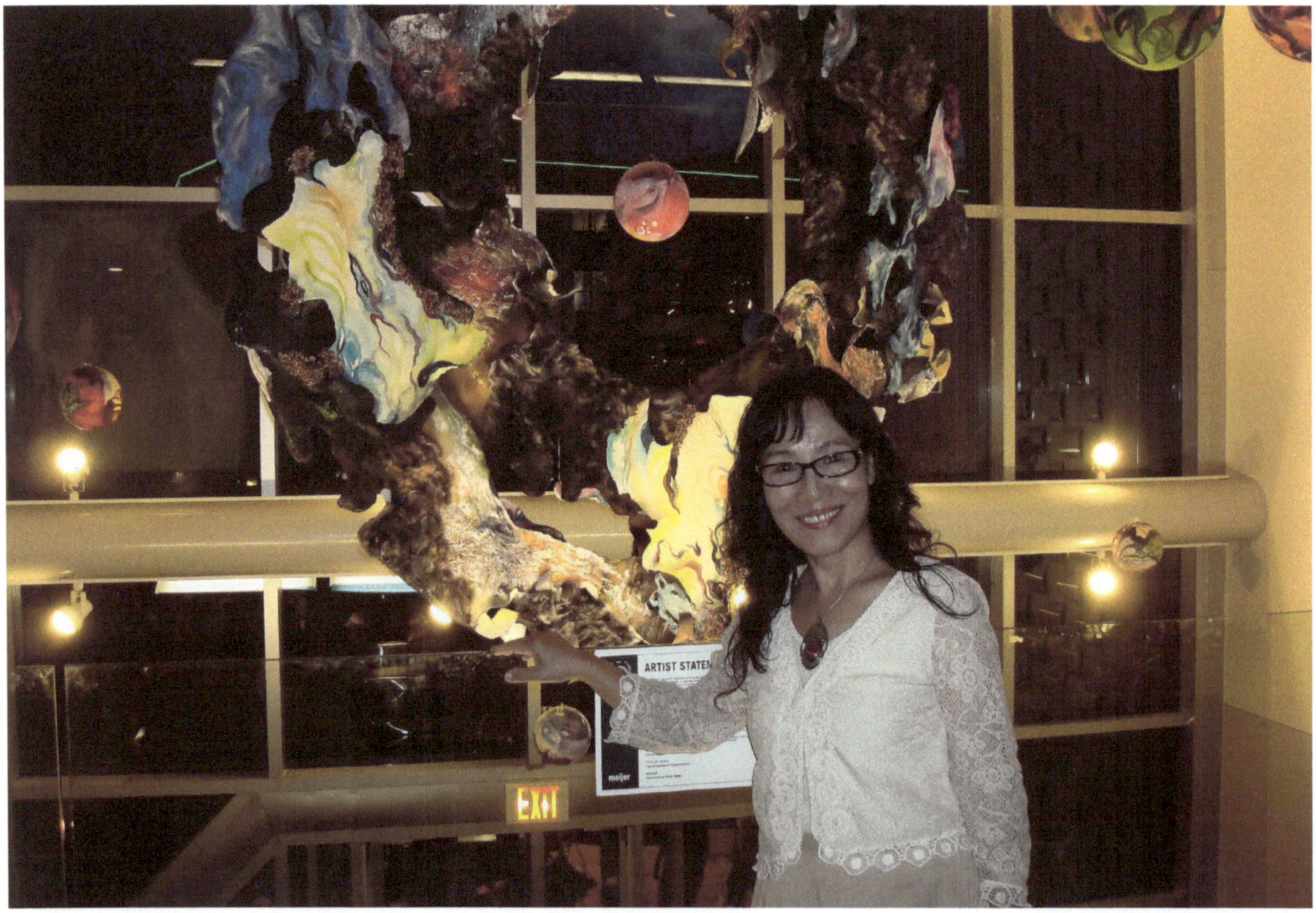
ARTIST
meijer
EXIT

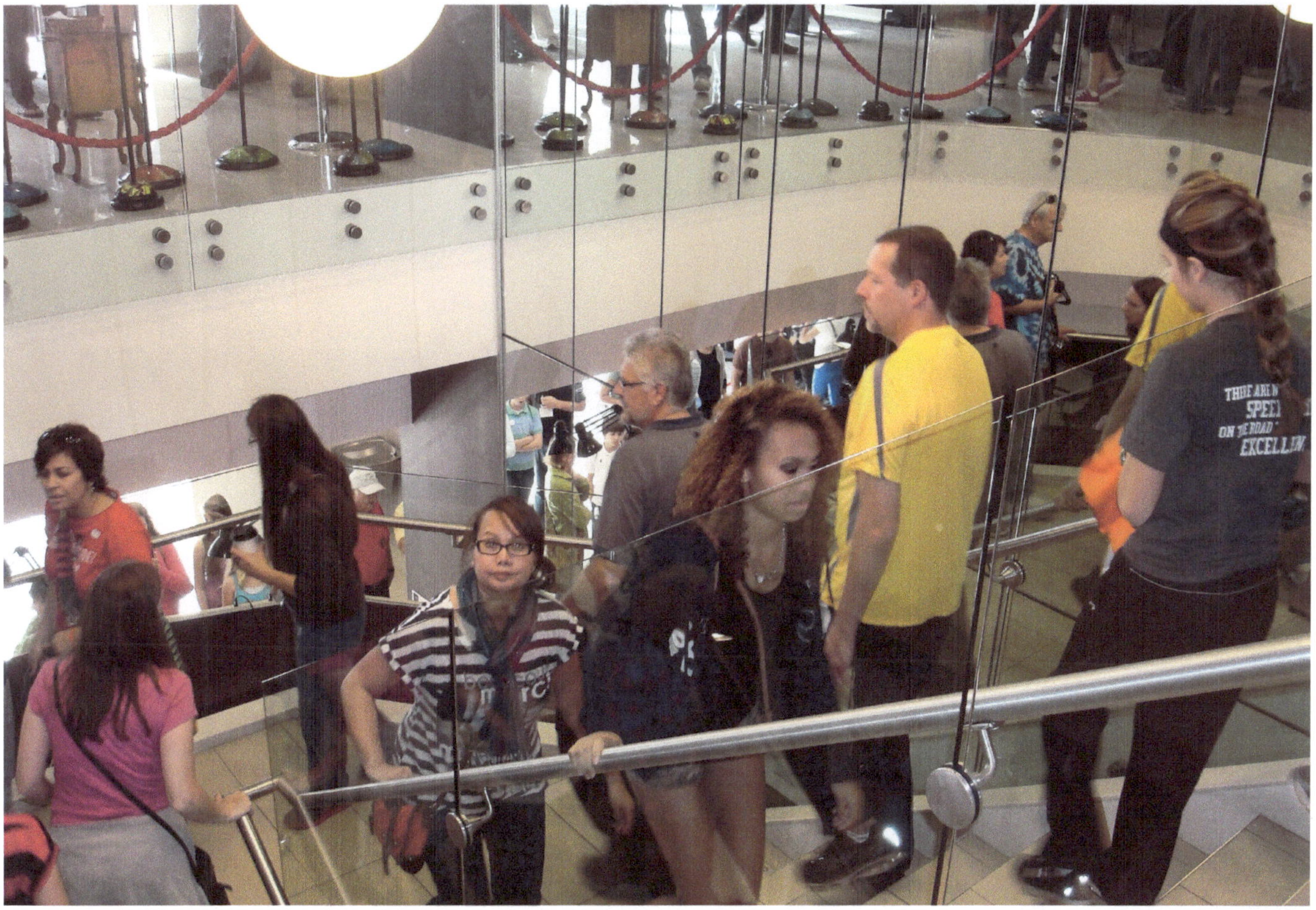

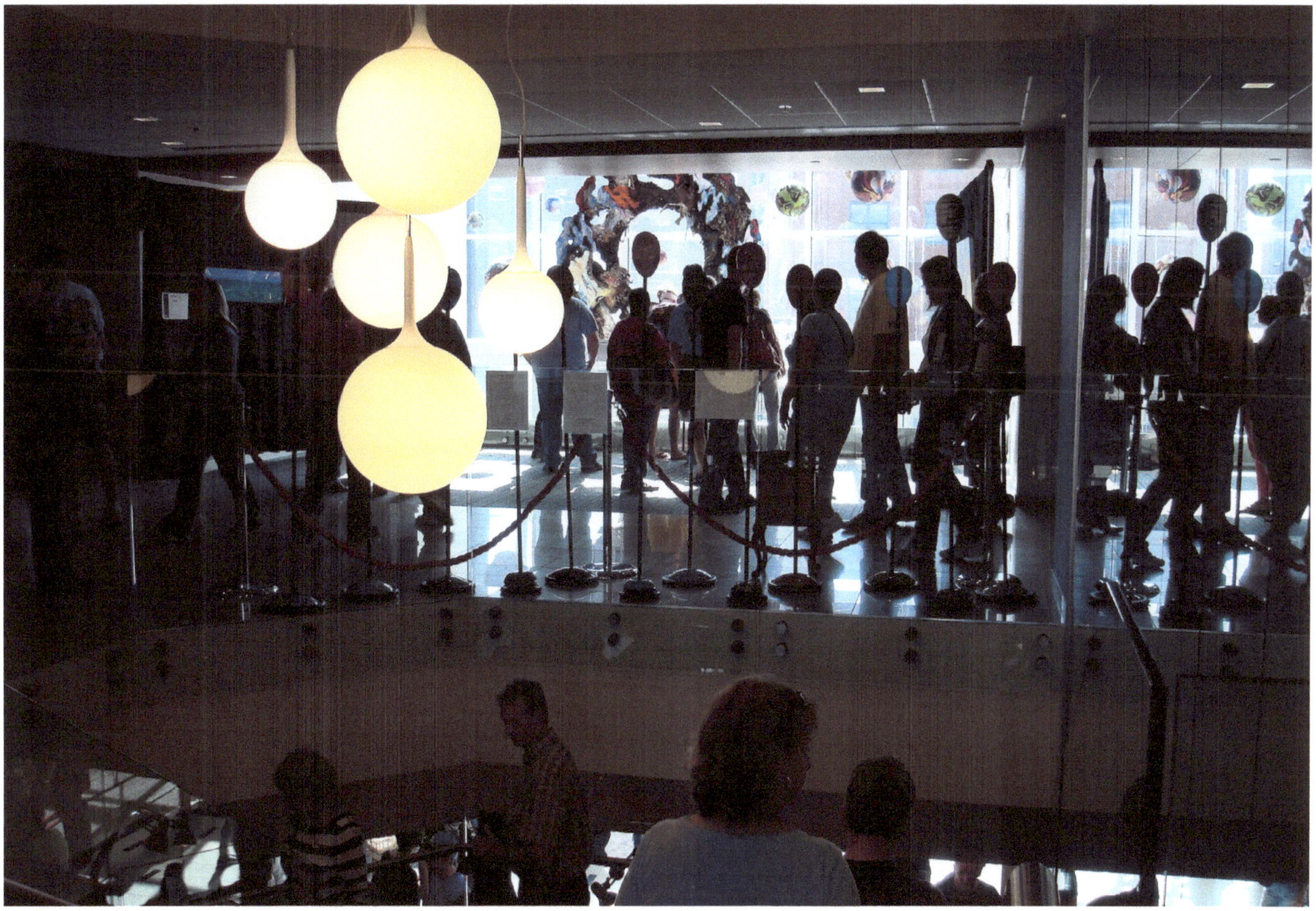

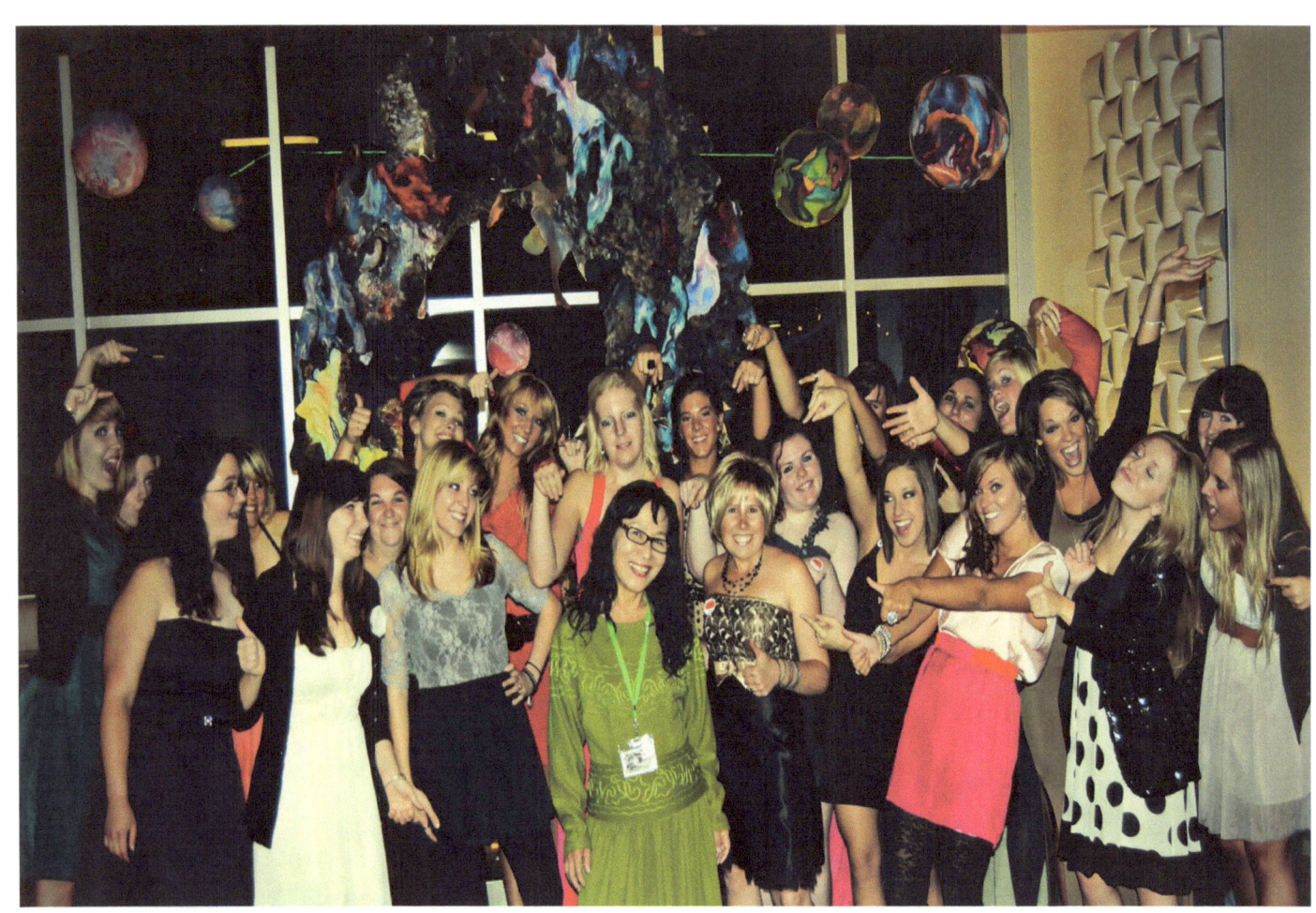

Photo from unknown sender by email 2012

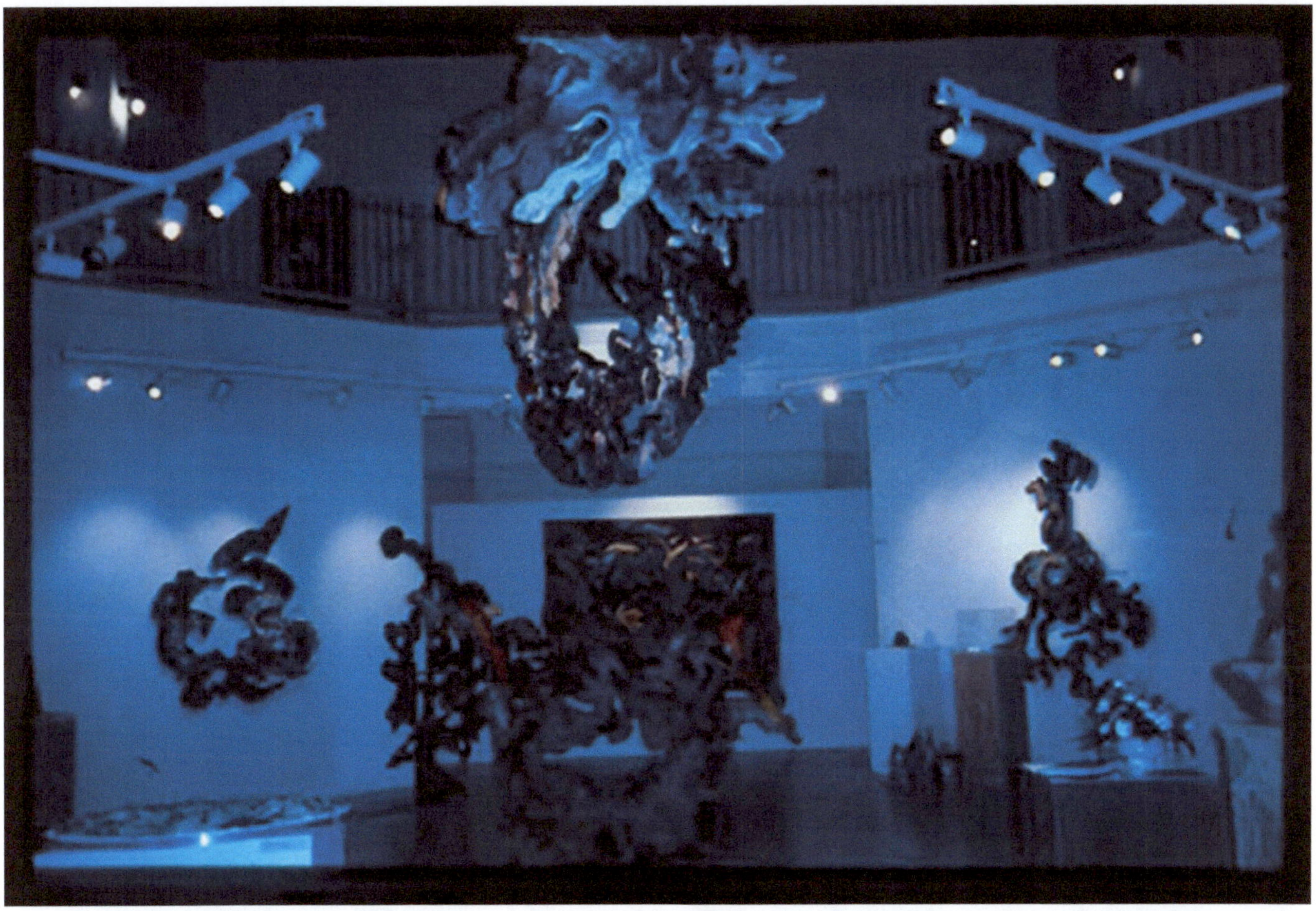

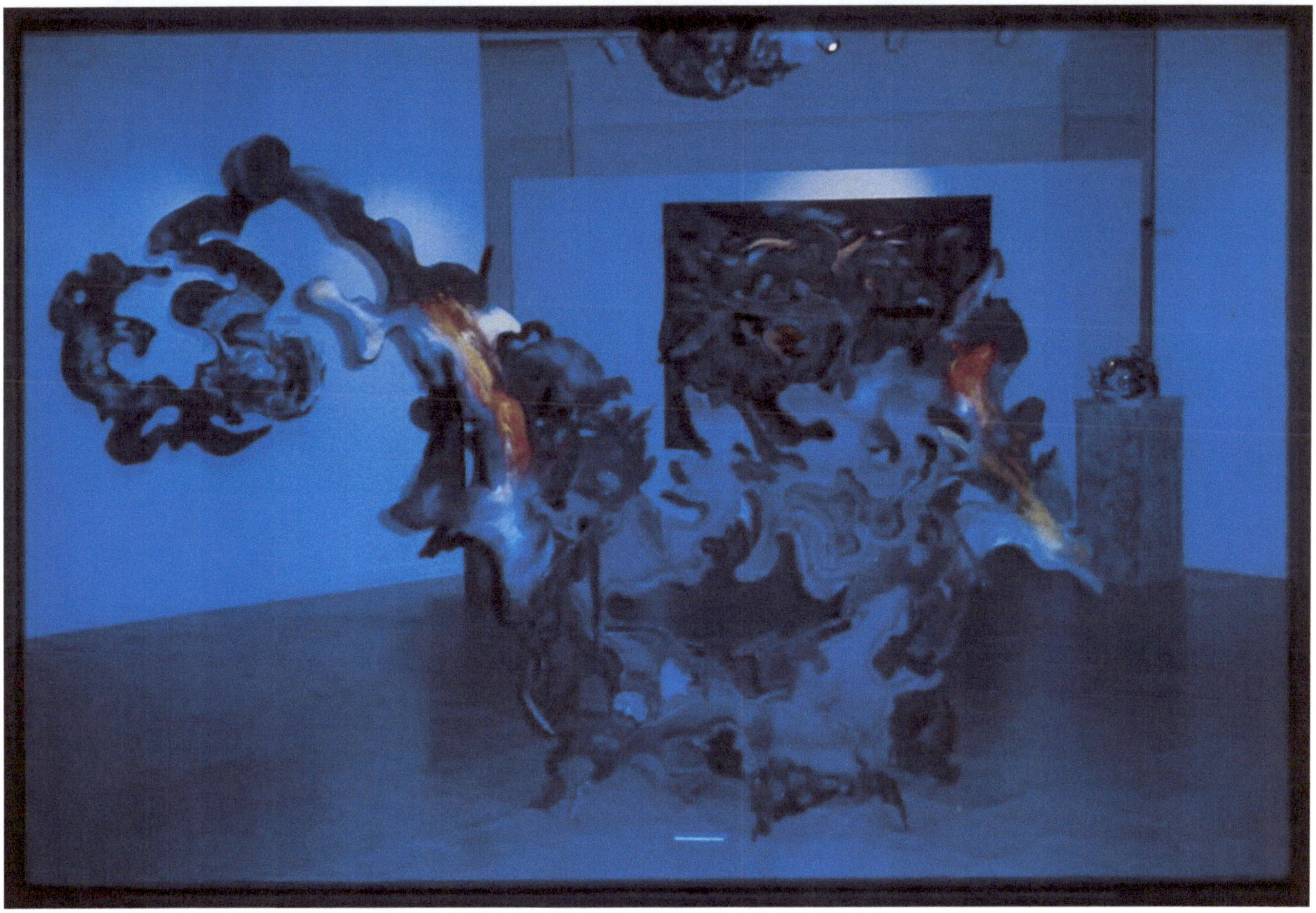

Rotunda Gallery, Western Michigan University

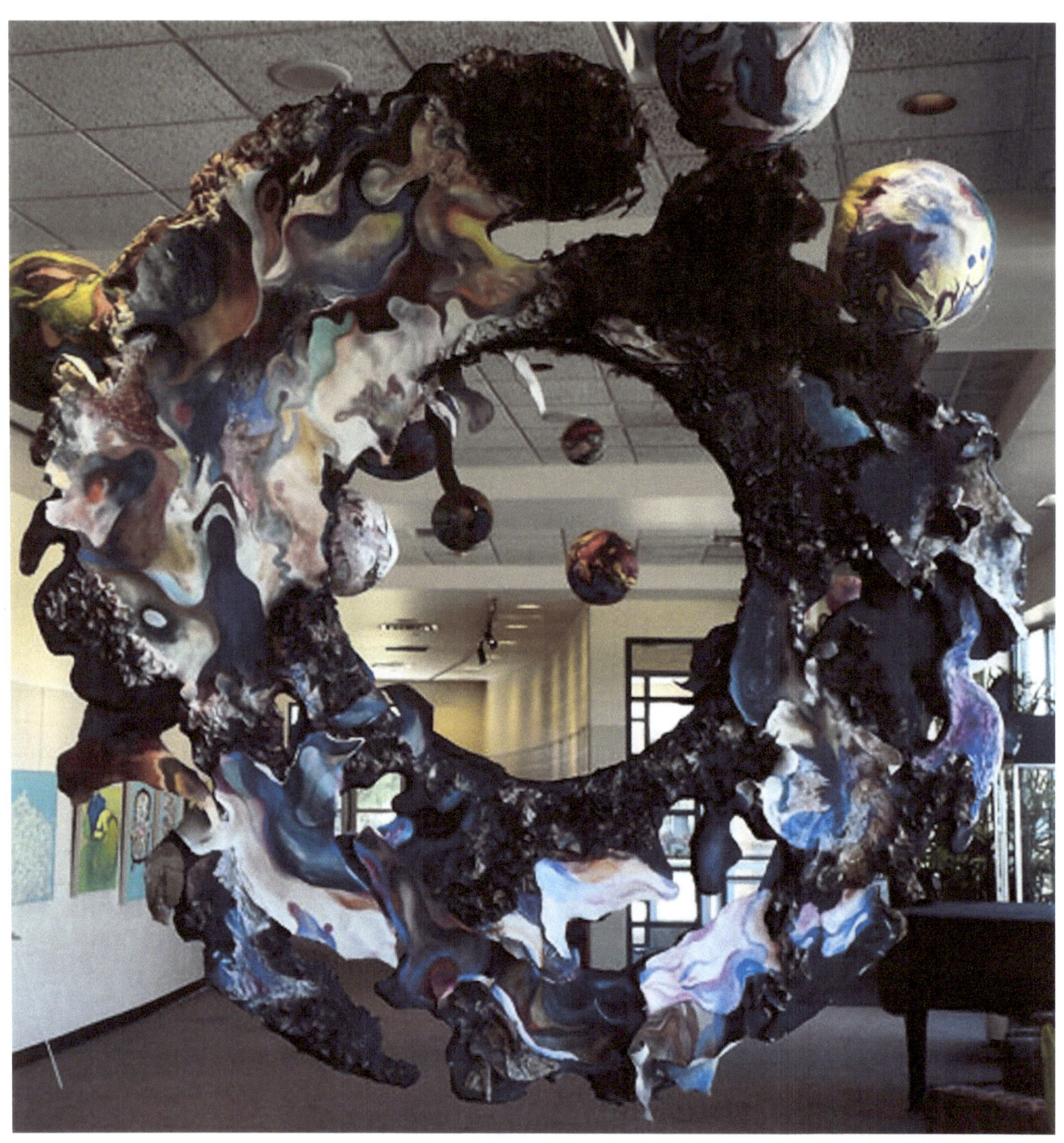

VanSingel Fine Arts Center, 2013

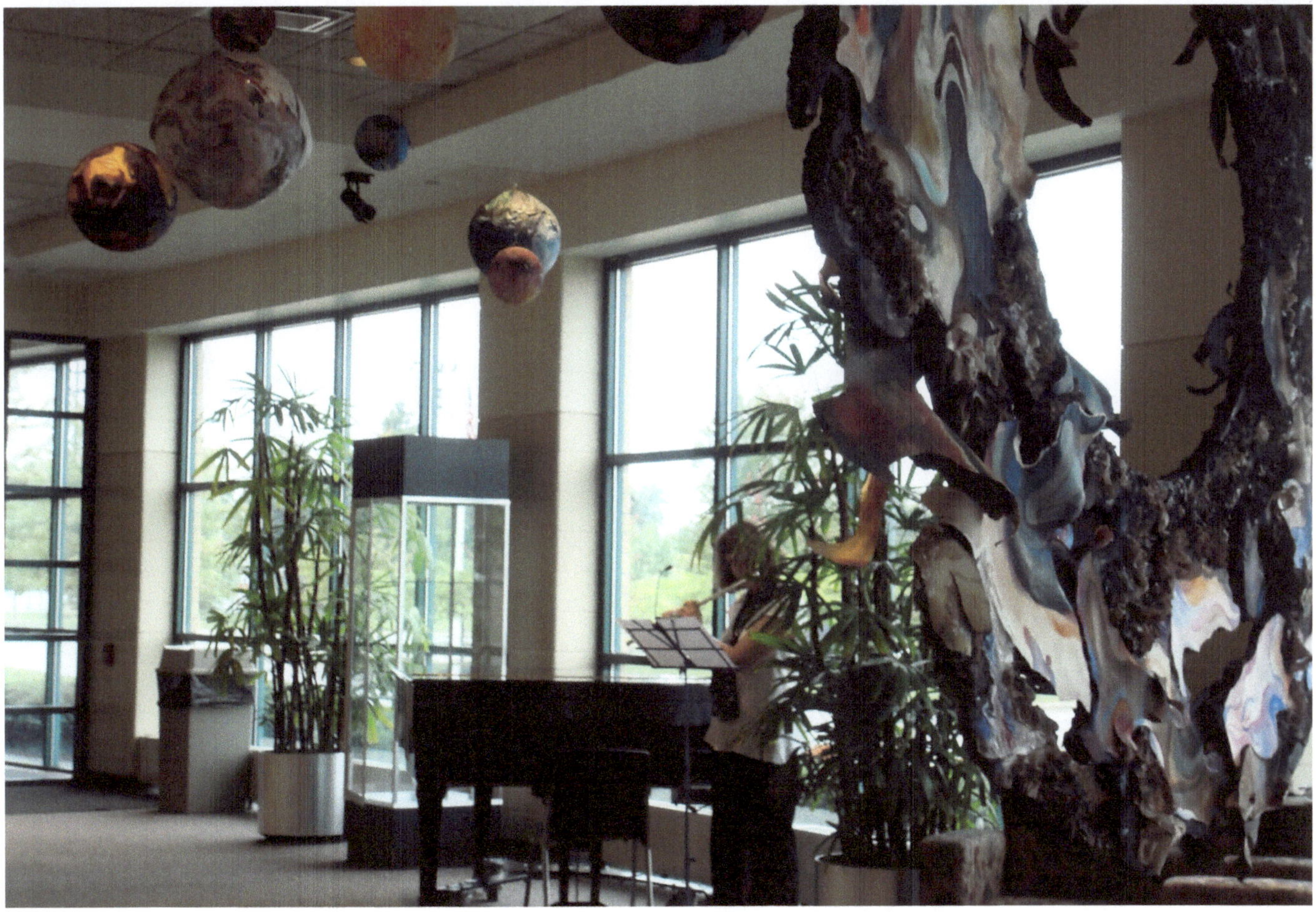

Flute Player: Aline Snoeyink

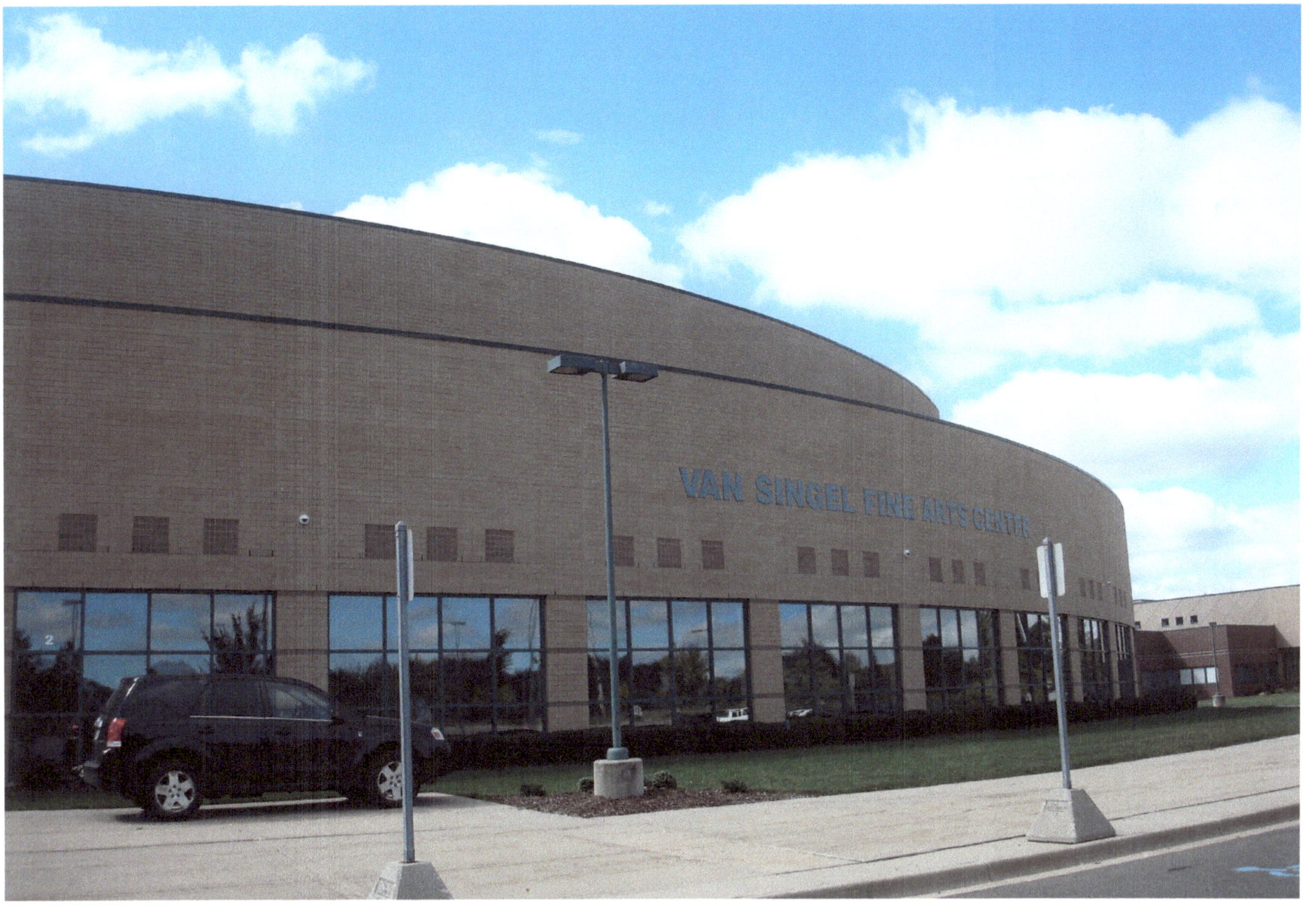

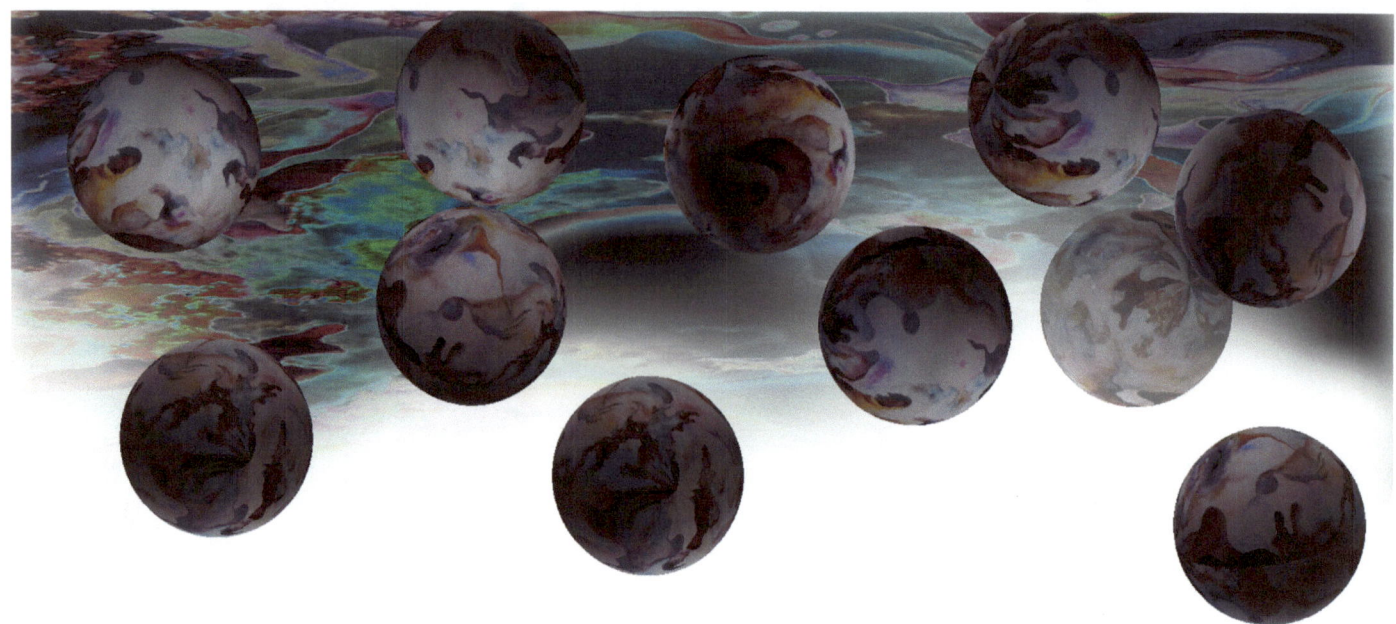

I have come to an acute realization how crucial and vital is human to express in life. Being able to communicate using language, a culturally acquired symbol, is an ability that is unique to humans. Language, however, by the virtue of its nature, is limited by cultural boundaries; one has to learn it to communicate.

However, unlike language, can transmit feelings and ideas evoking them through lines, shapes, texture, arrangement and/or colors, on a two/three dimensional space. My love for, interest in, and an innate aptitude in the visual arts inevitably determined the artistic medium by which I am to "express" my life. It can transcend temporal and spatial boundaries; it speaks universal human "language." - InSoon -

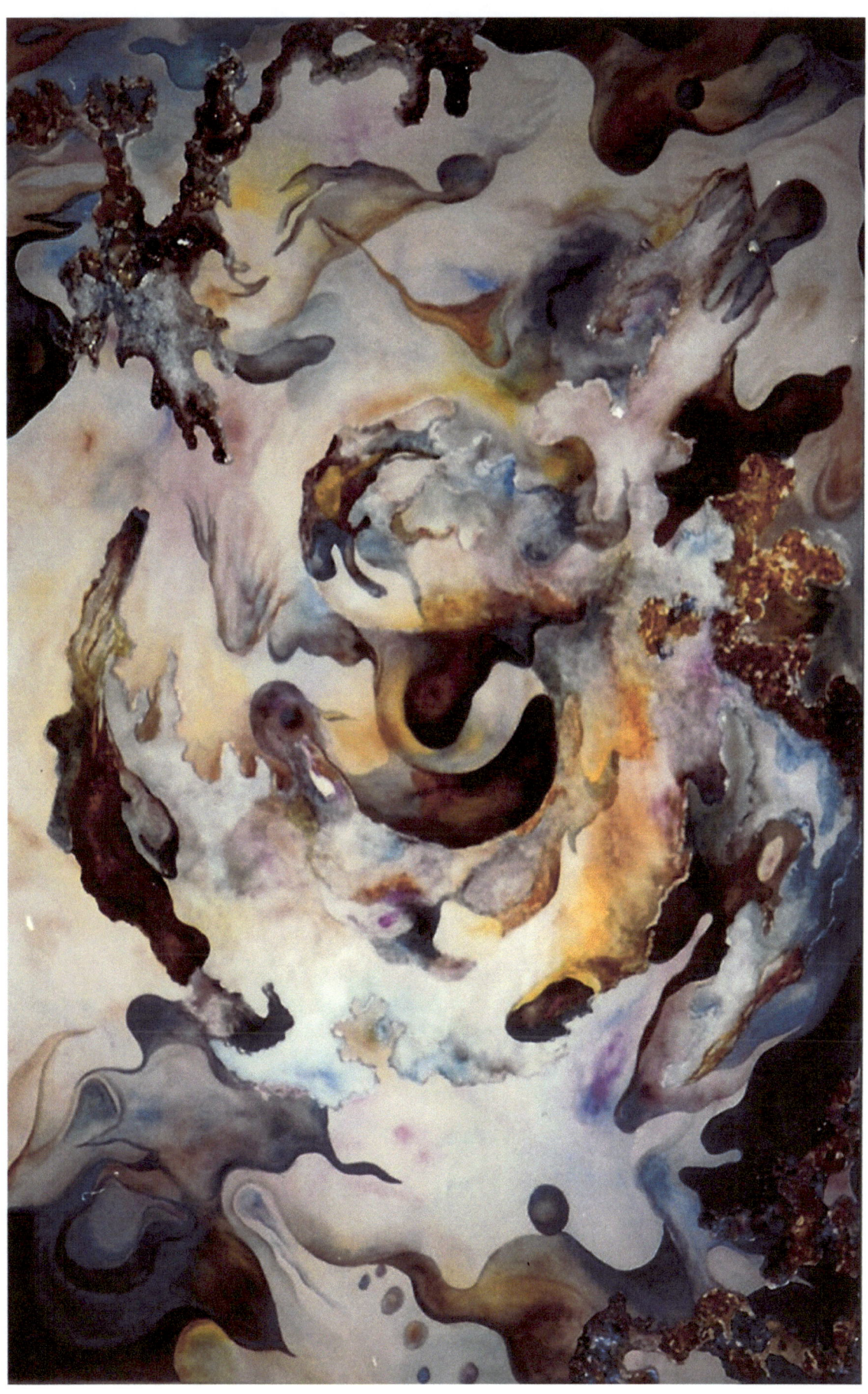

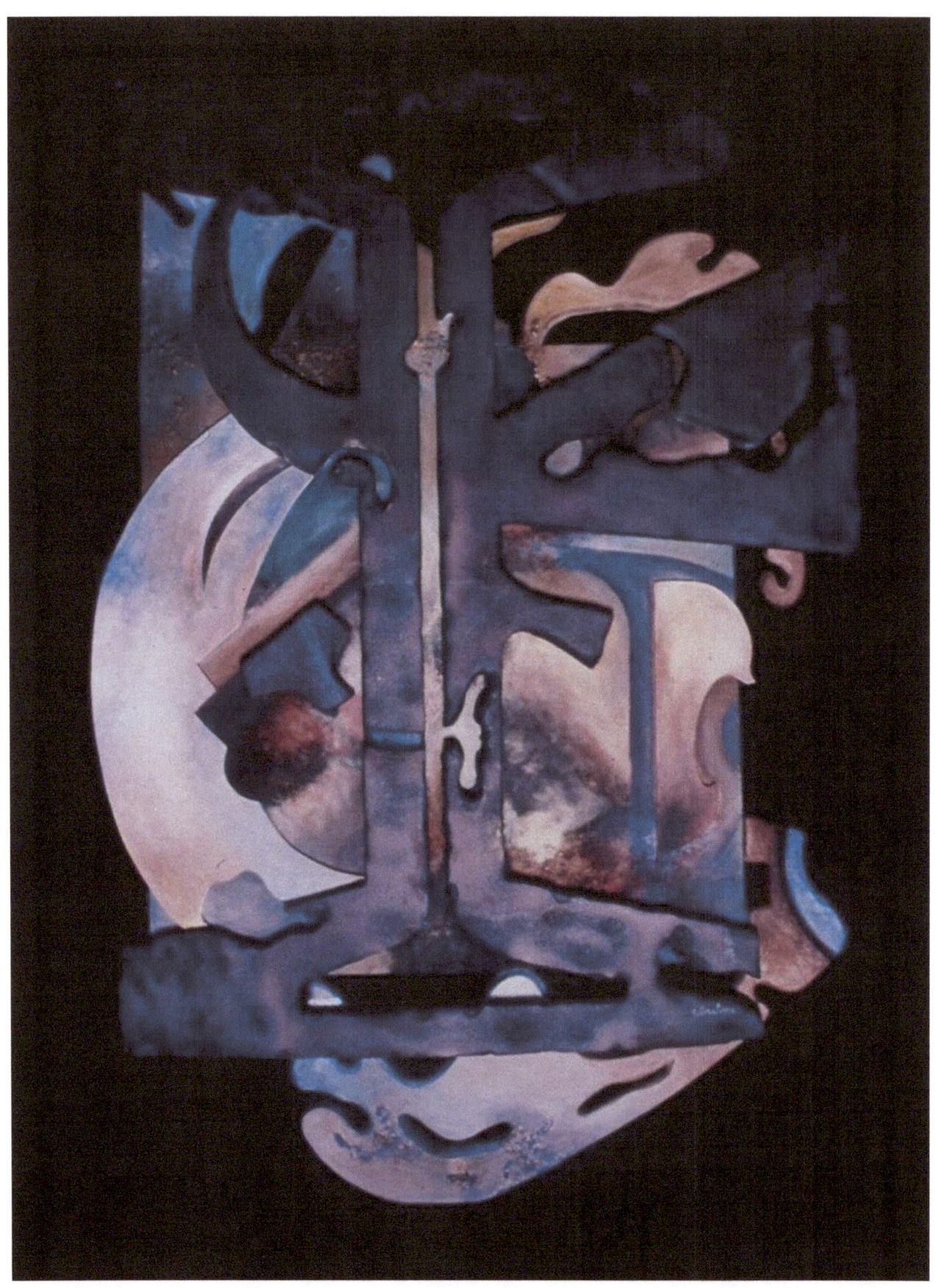

Fortuitous

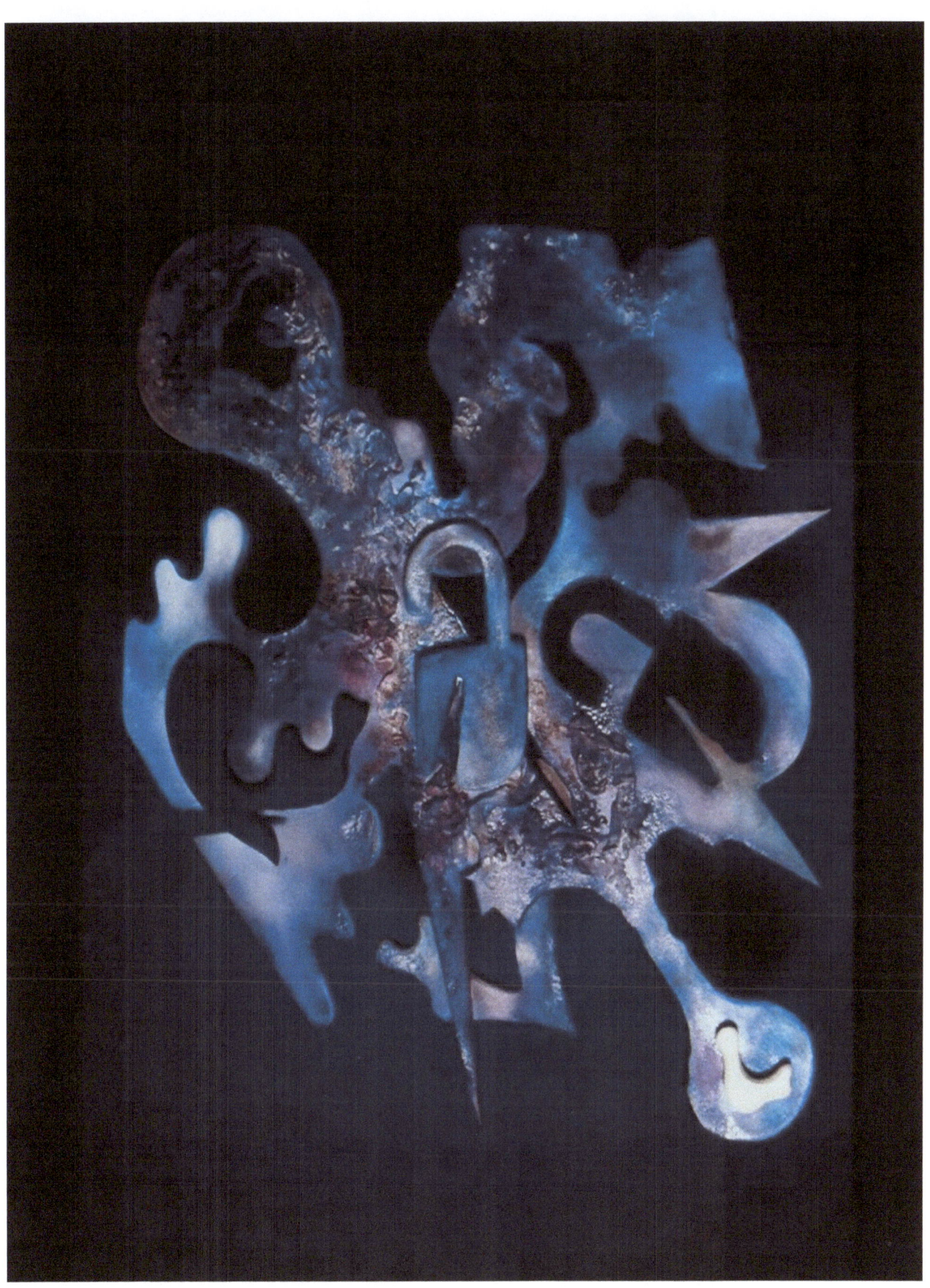

Positive & Negative

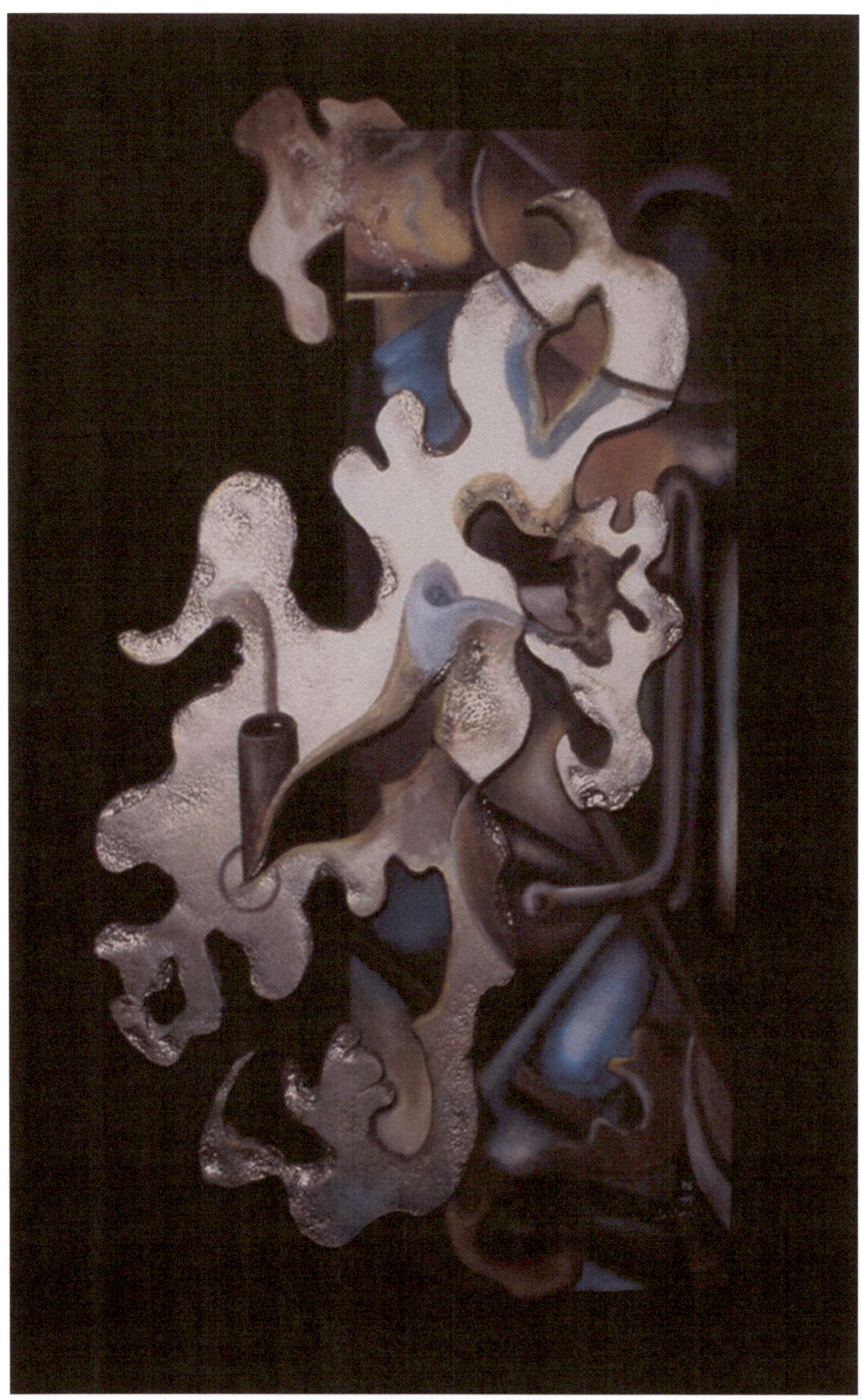

Intuition

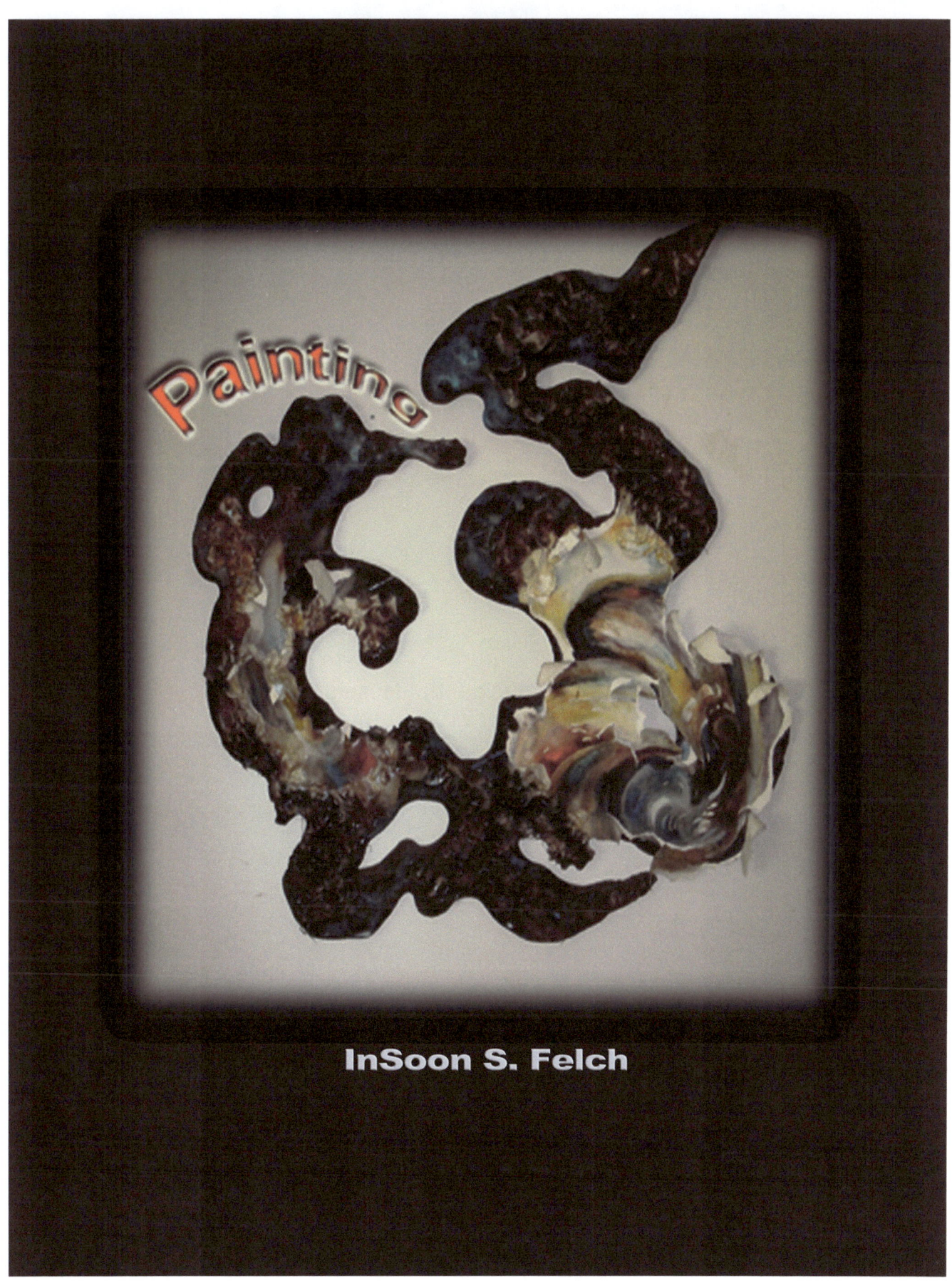

InSoon S. Felch

The Pursuit of Happiness

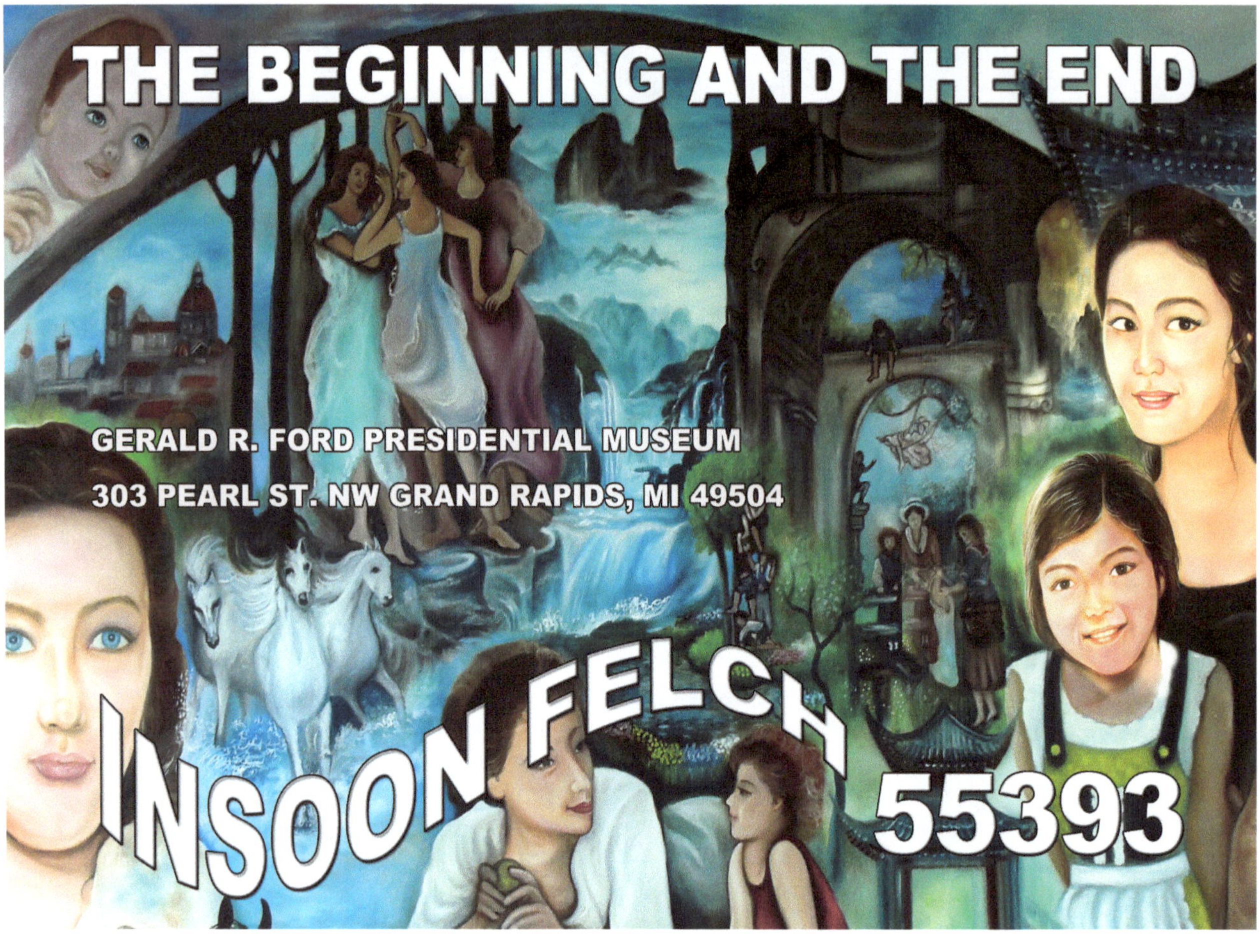

THE BEGINNING AND THE END

GERALD R. FORD PRESIDENTIAL MUSEUM

303 PEARL ST. NW GRAND RAPIDS, MI 49504

INSOON FELCH

55393

Gerald R. Ford Presidential Museum 2013

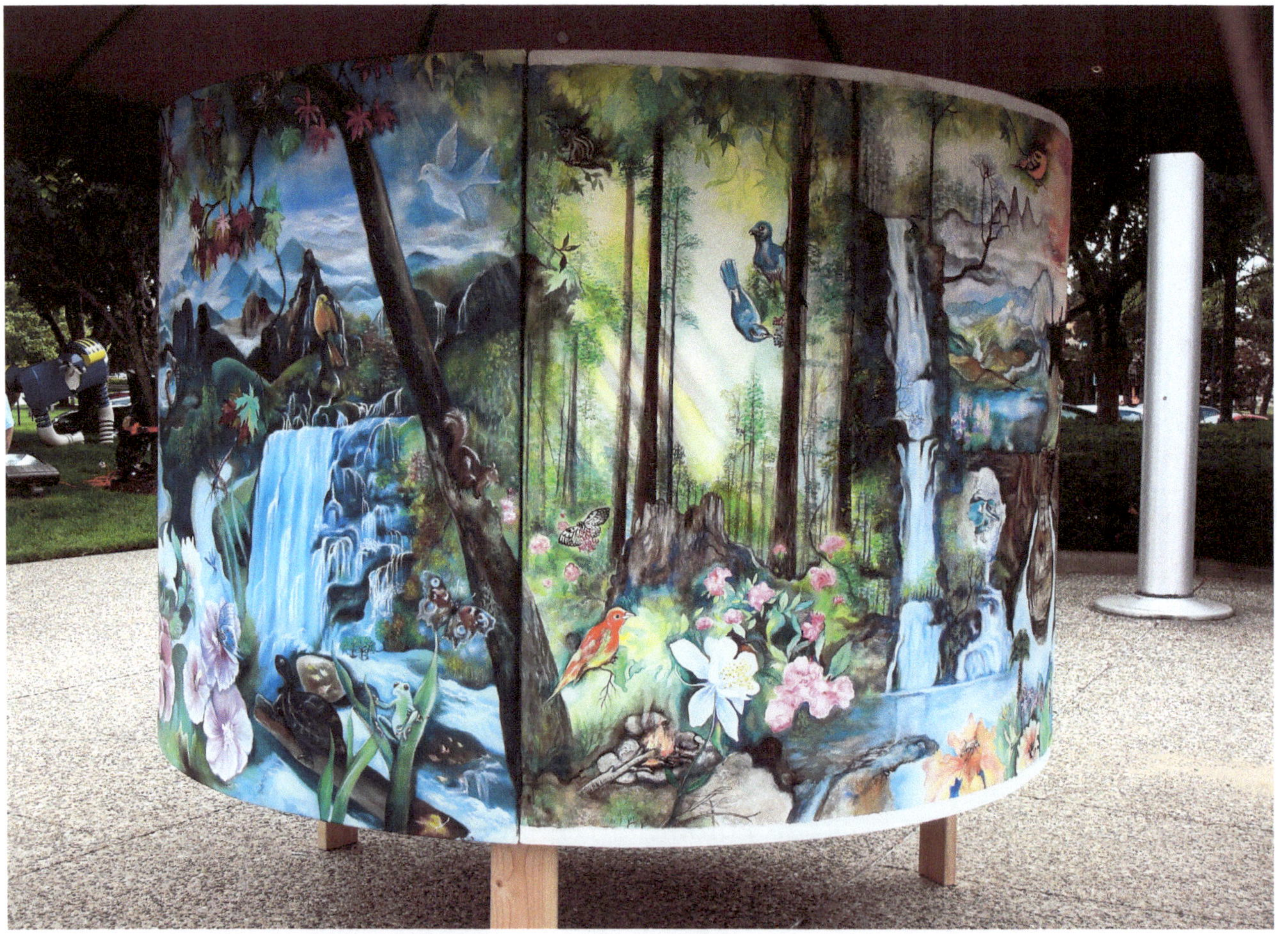

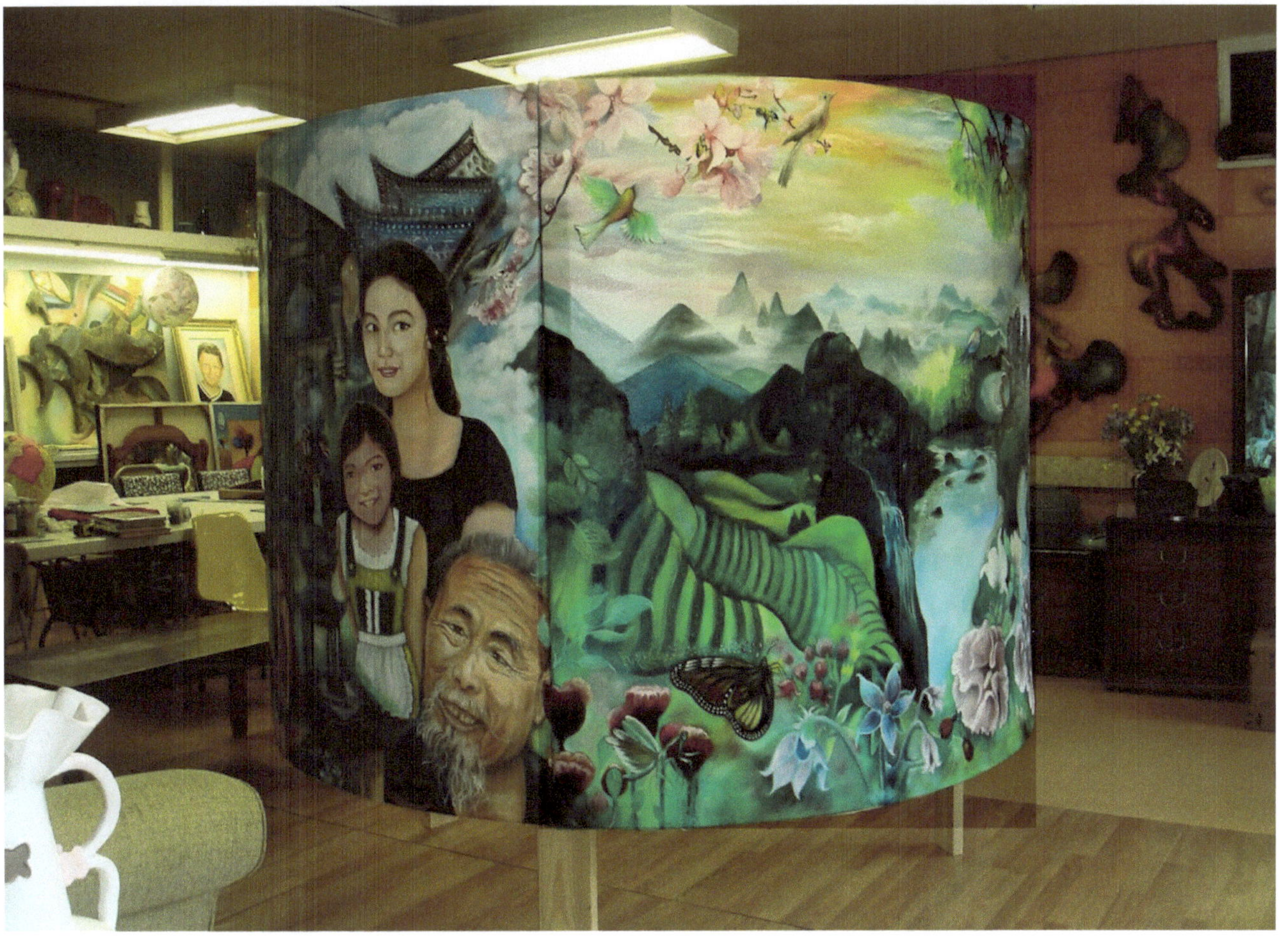

InSoon's Art Gallery & Studio Vs. Gerald R. Ford Presidential Museum, 2013

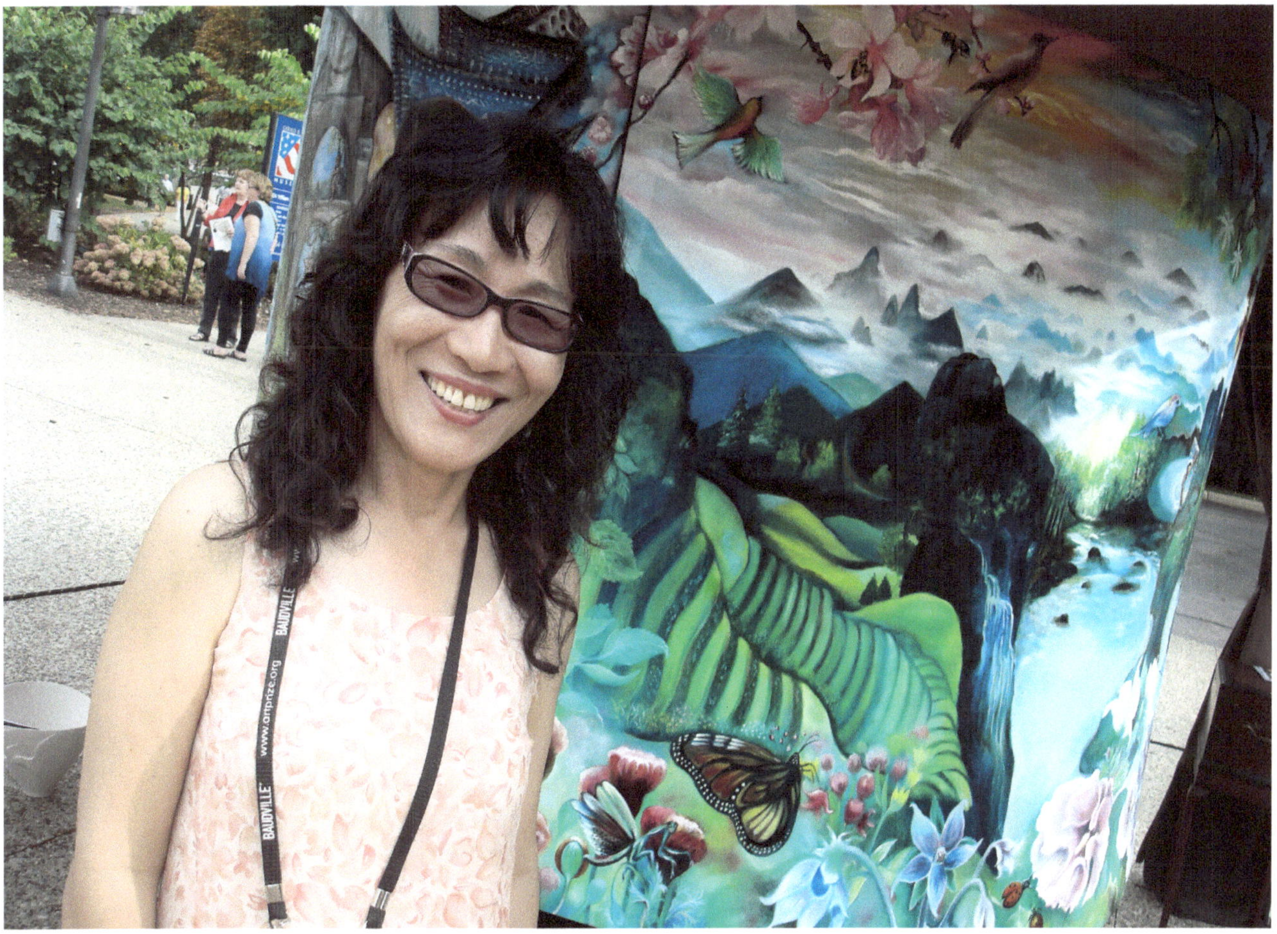

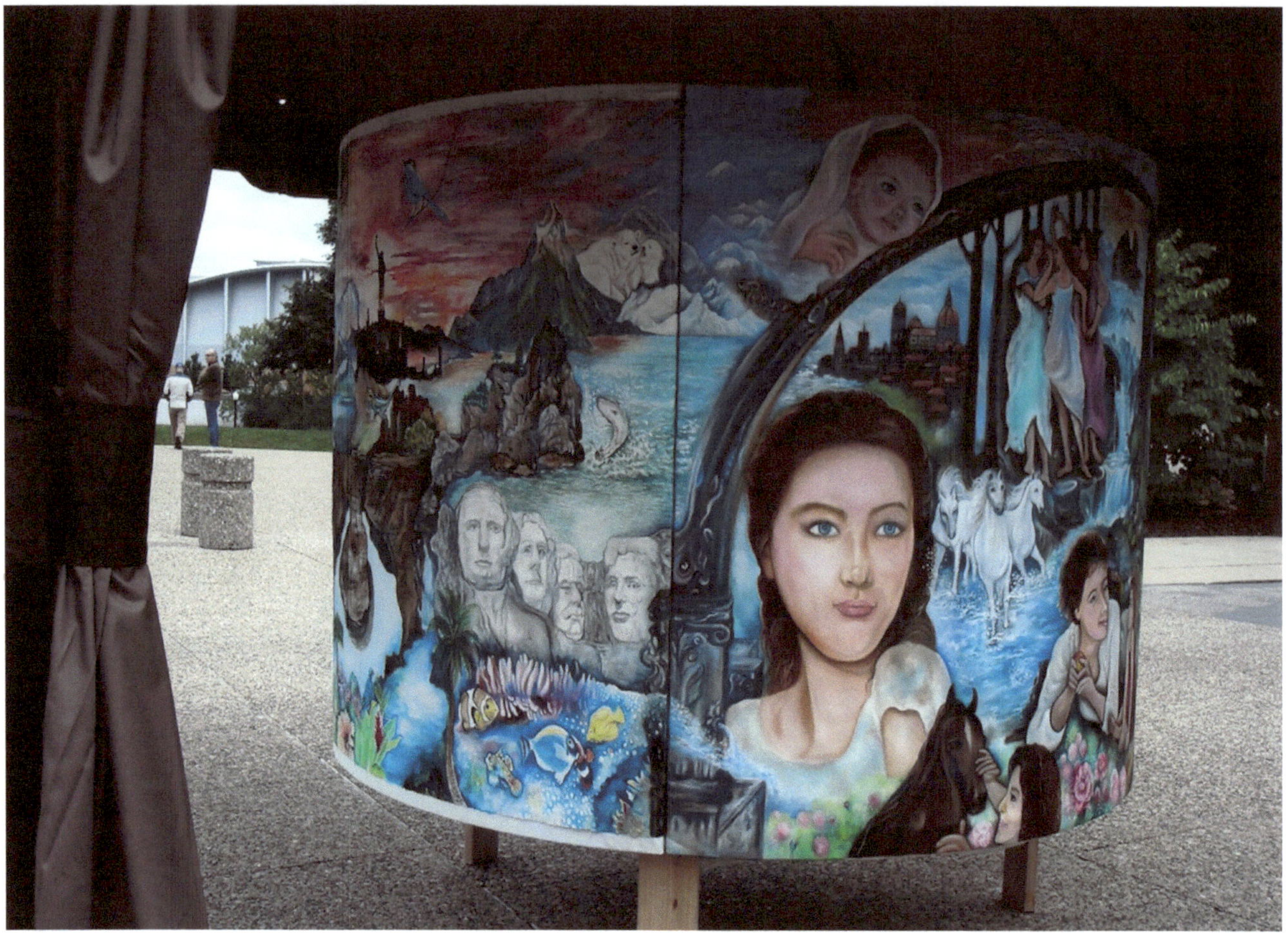

Outdoor Vs. Indoor Exhibition

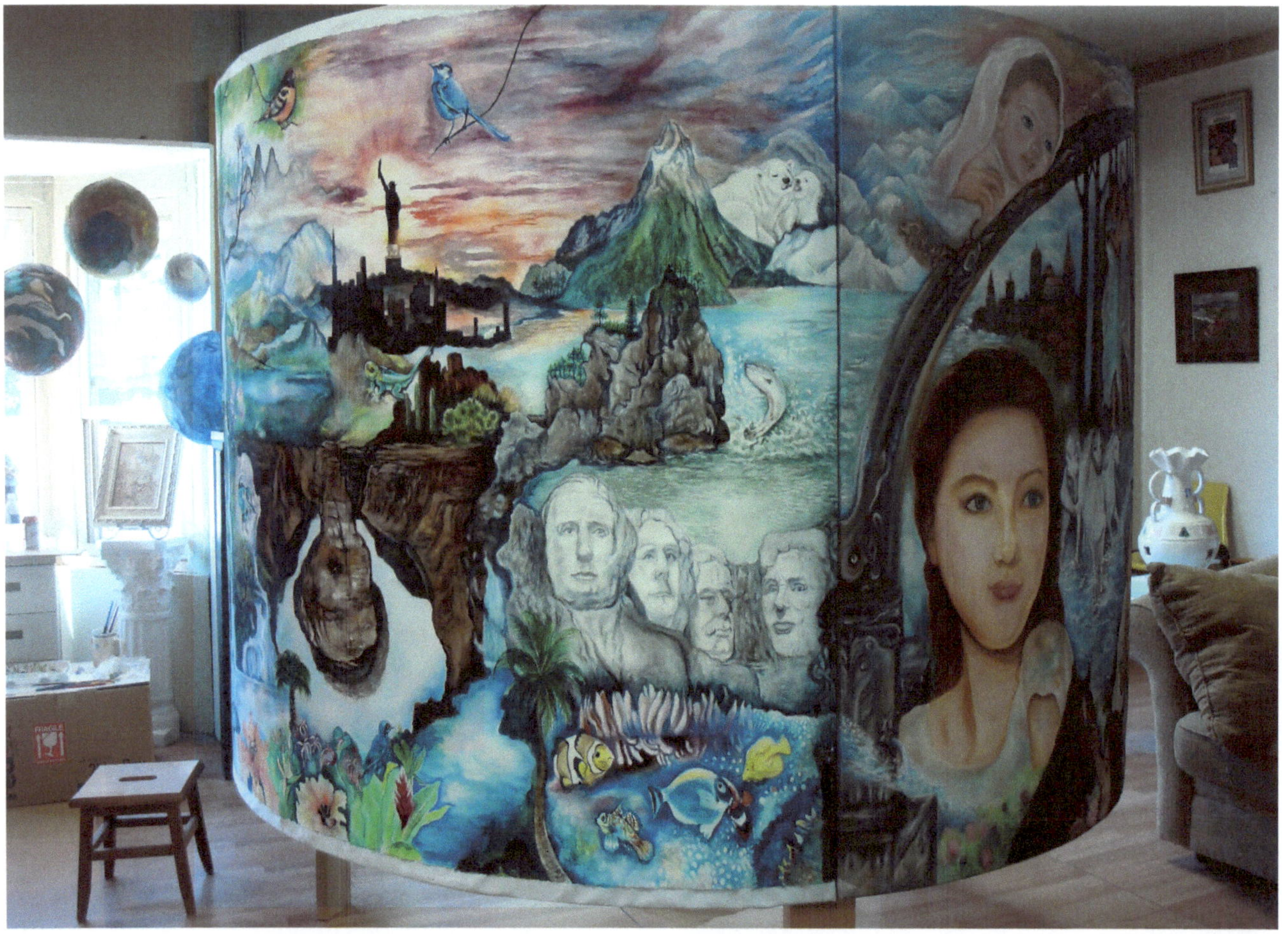

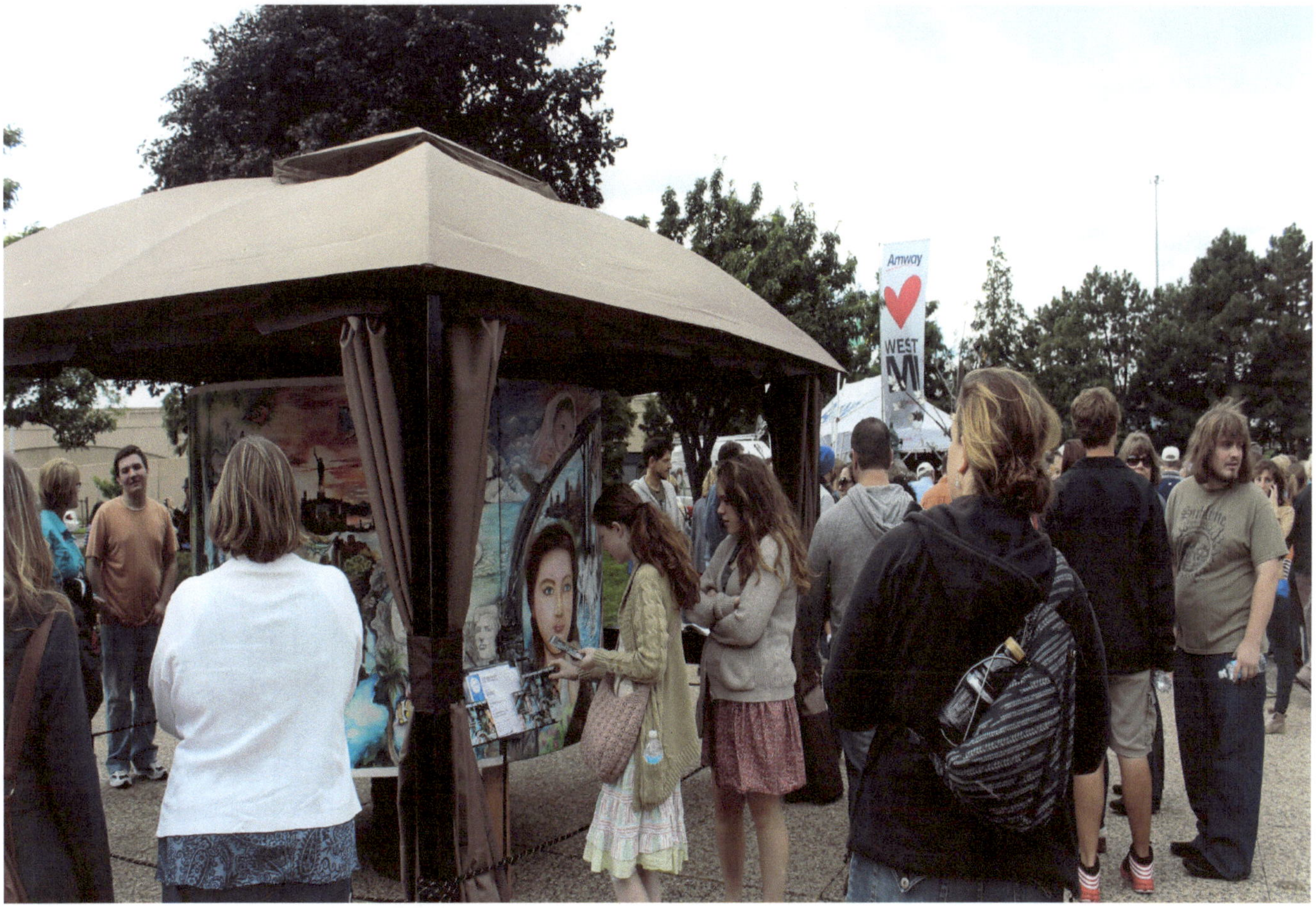

Gerald R. Ford Presidential Museum, 2013

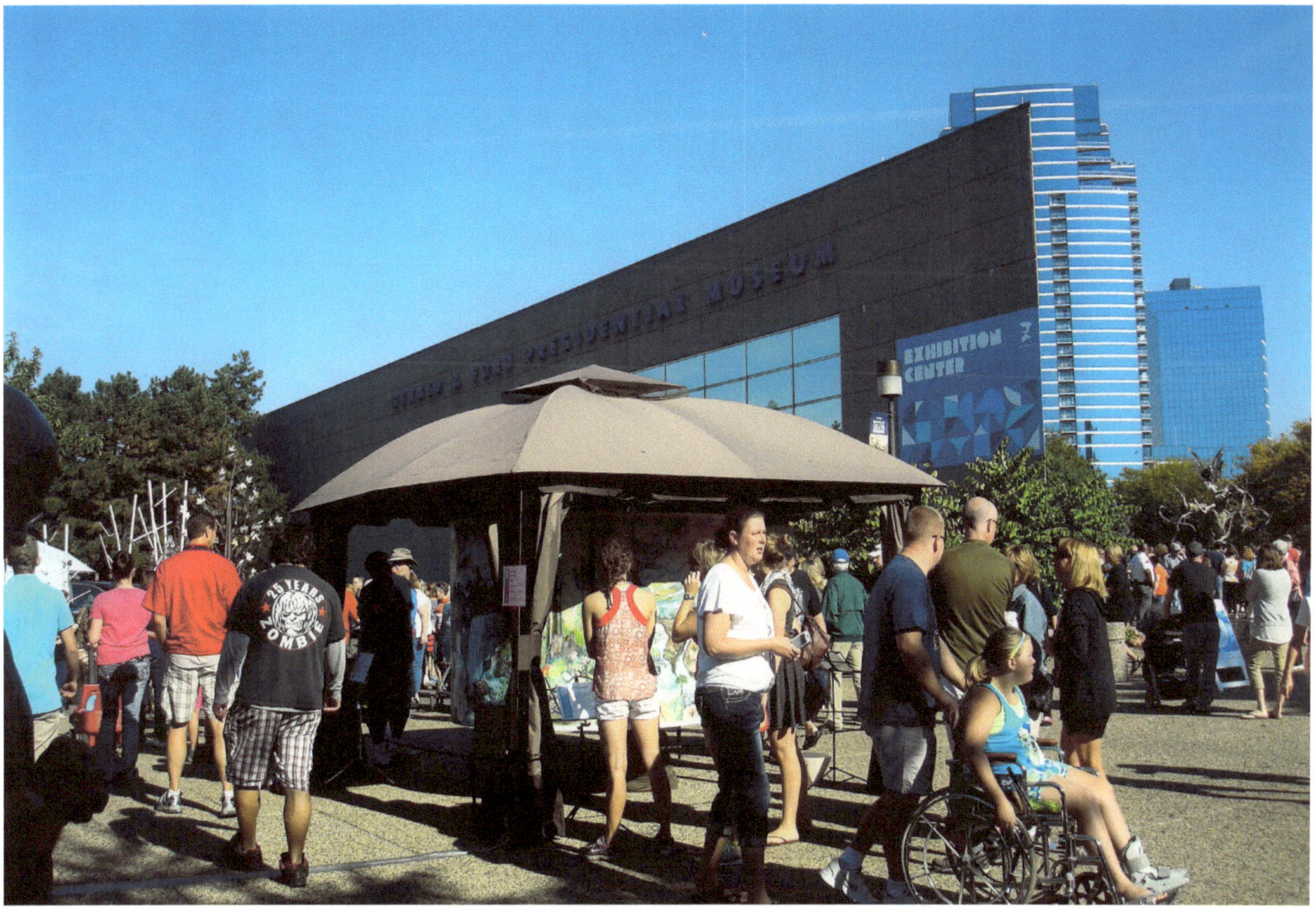

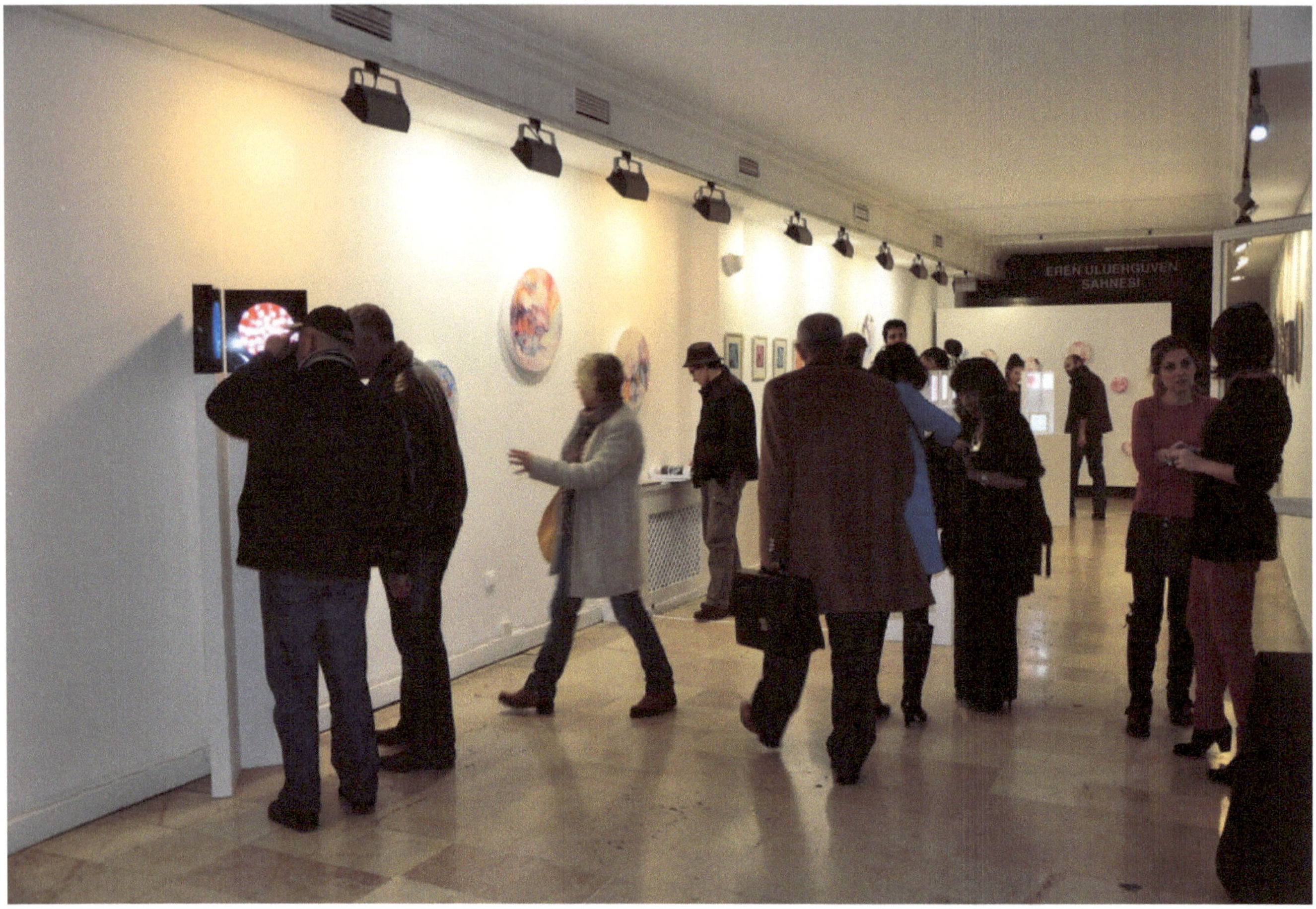

Mutuality/Realization, Pera Gallery, Istanbul Turkey, 2013

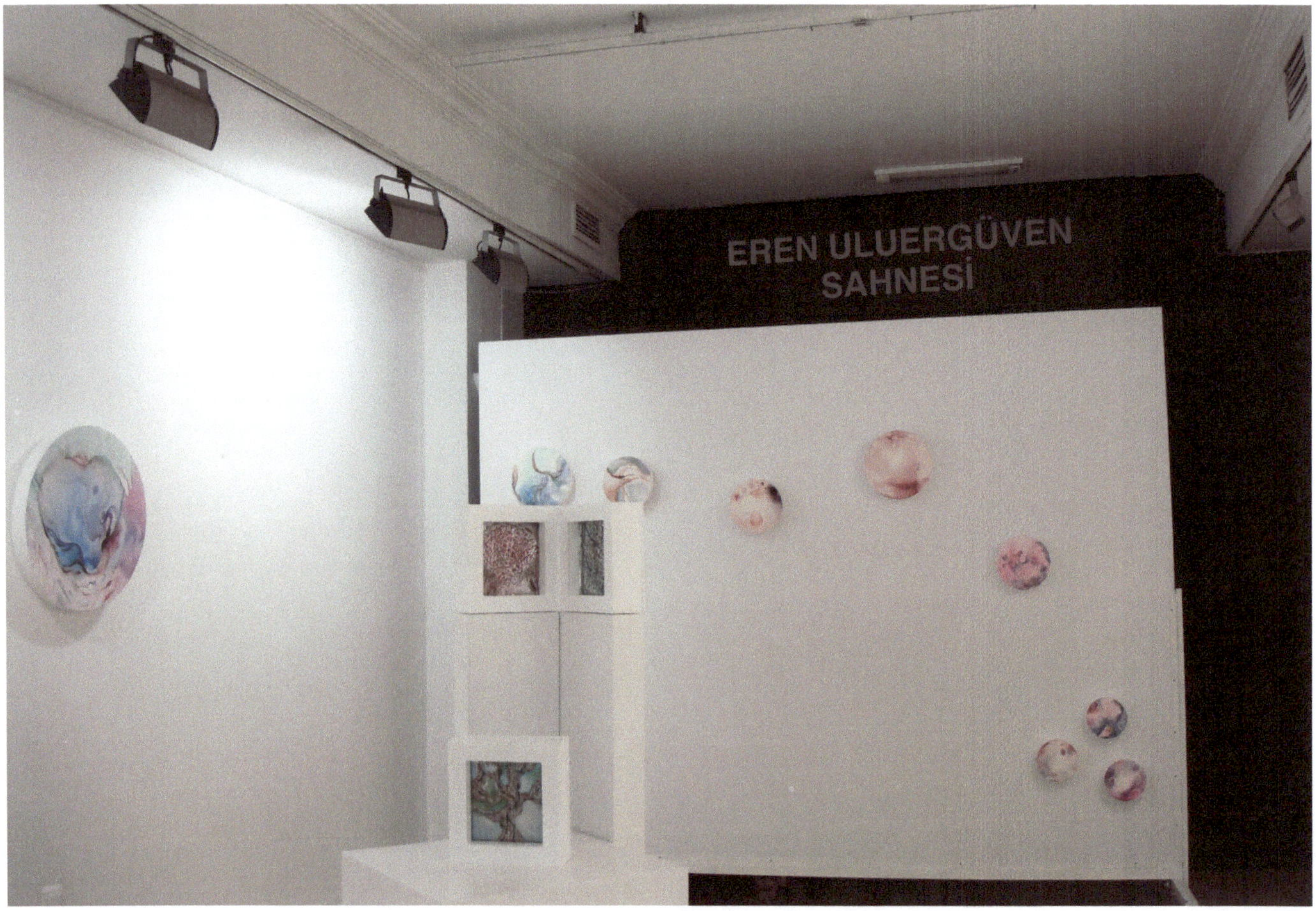

pera sanat galerisi

21 Şubat
17 Mart 2013

Açılış ve Kokteyl : 21 Şubat 2013 – Saat: 18.00

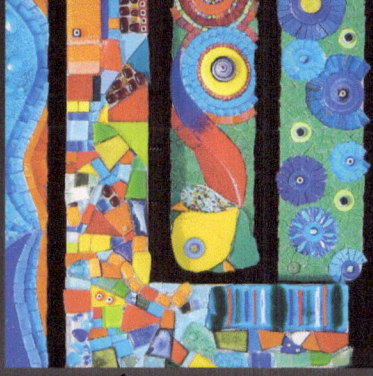

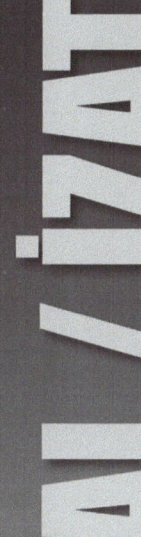

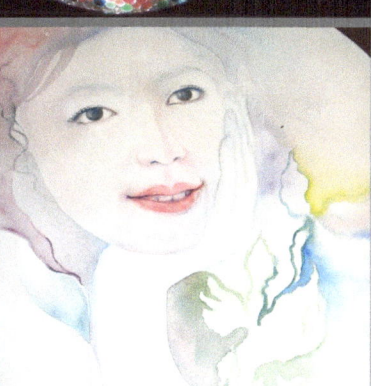

MITUAL / IZATION
Mutuality/ / Realization

BANU BİLGİNER
İNSOON FELCH
SUNSOOK ROH

Curator: Nilüfer MOAYERİ

www.peraartgallery.com

Sıraselviler Cad. No.26 Taksim/İstanbul Tel. 0212 245 3008 Faks. 0212 252 3082
pera@peraartgallery.com | info@peraartgallery.com | art@peraartgallery.com

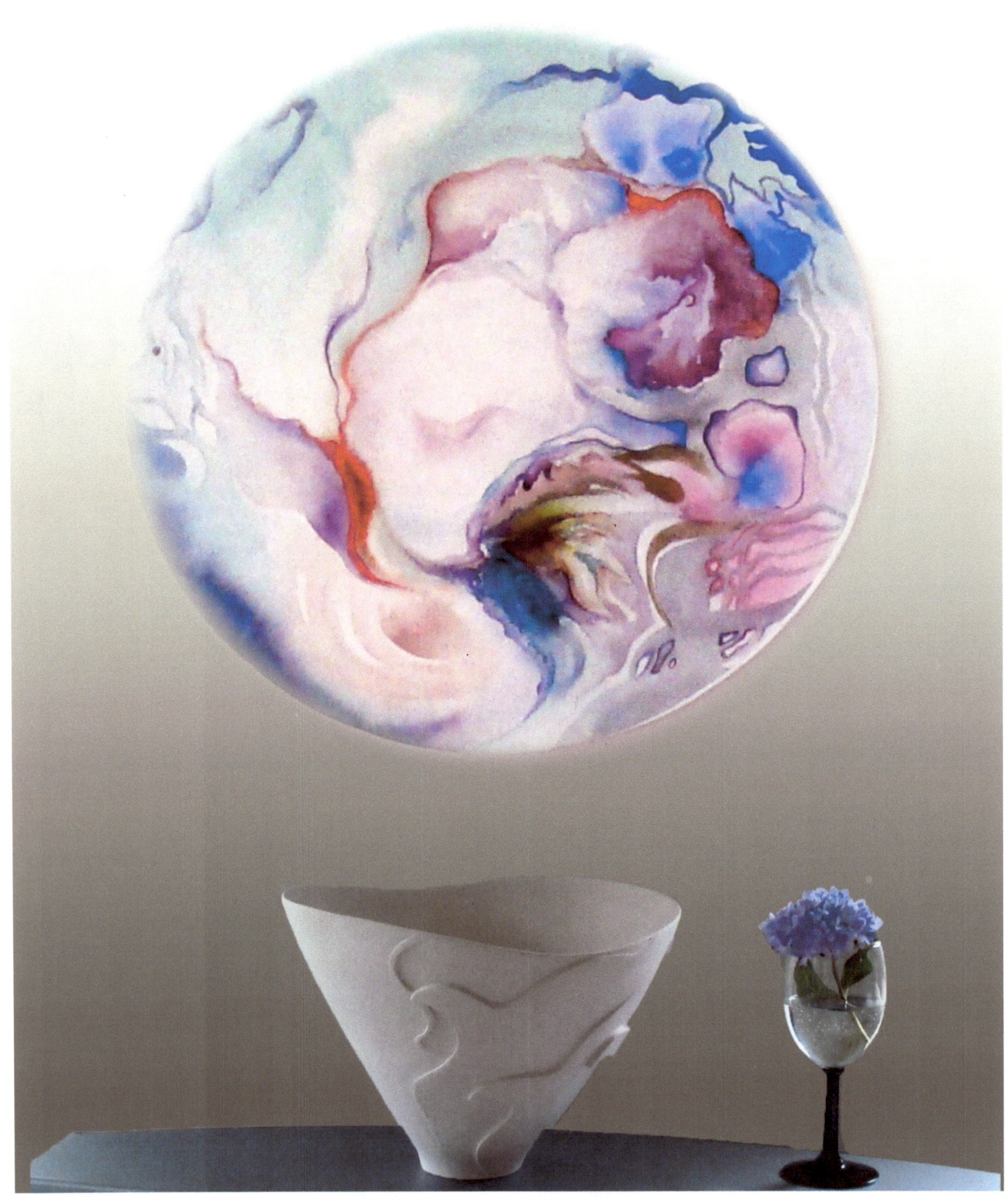

Istanbul, Turkey, 2013

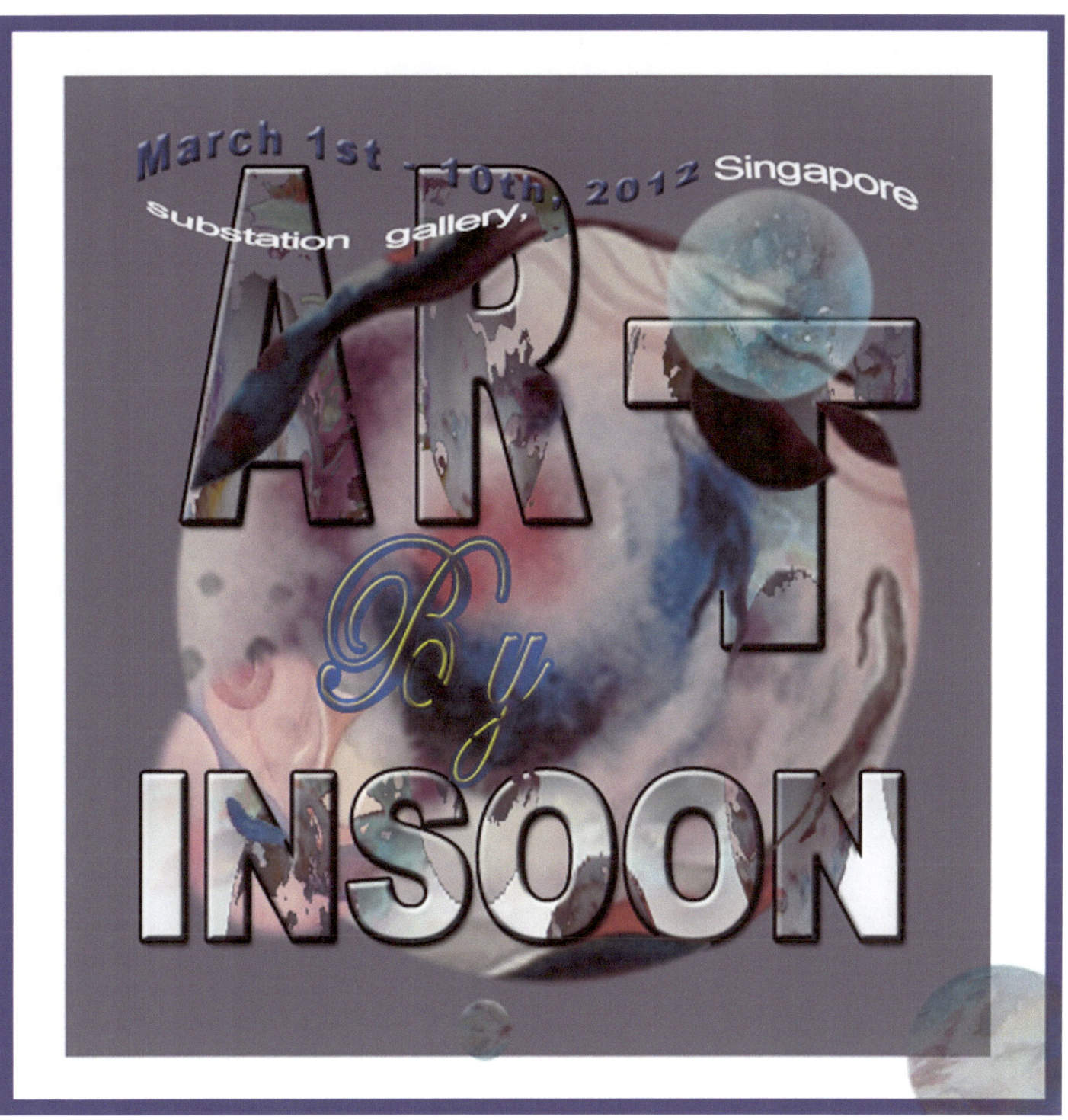

Solo Exhibition, Spatial Conflicts, Substation Gallery, Singapore, 2012

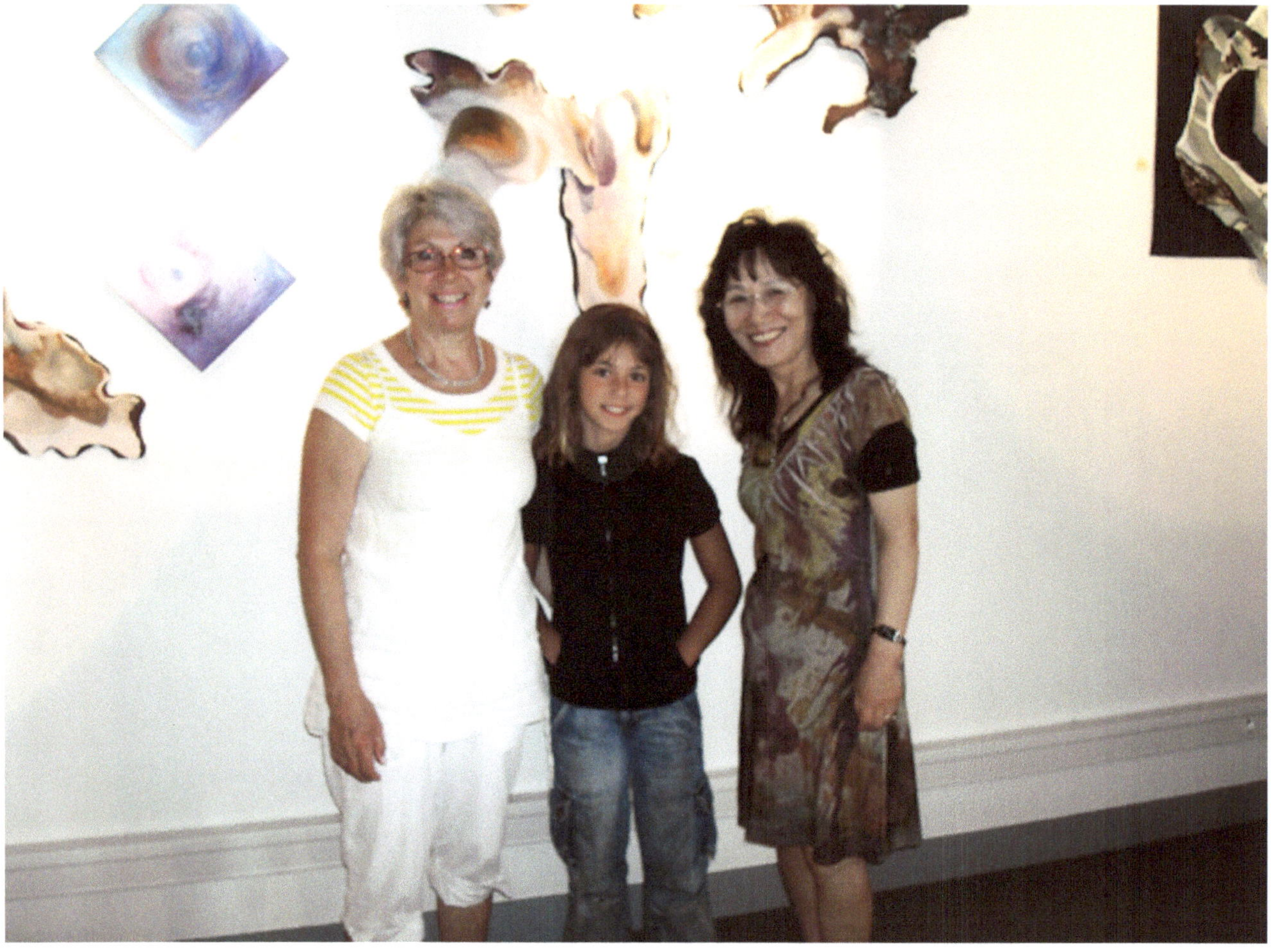

Invitational Solo Exhibition, France 2009 (With Visiting French Artist & Her Daughter)

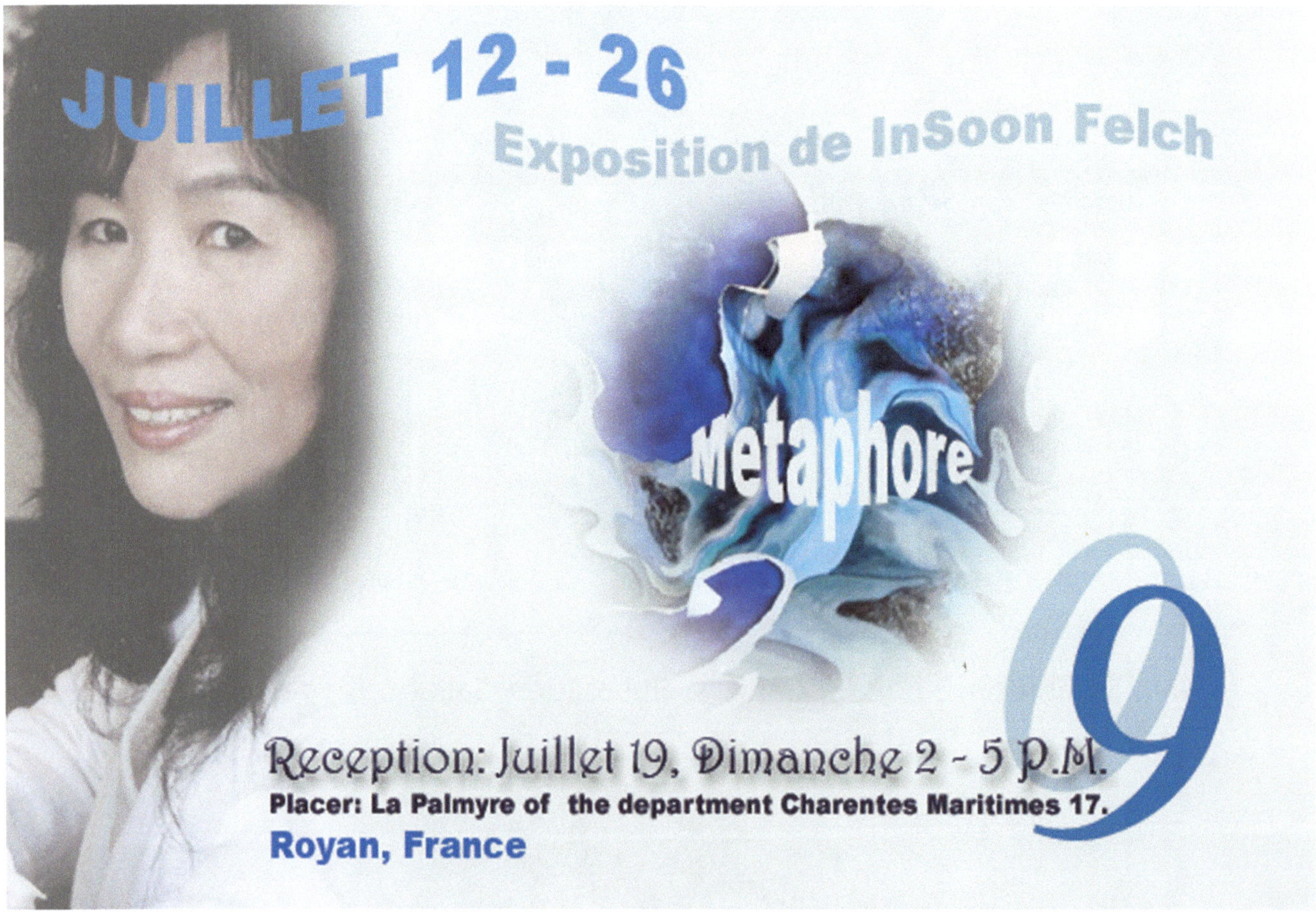

JUILLET 12 - 26
Exposition de InSoon Felch

Metaphore

09

Reception: Juillet 19, Dimanche 2 - 5 P.M.
Placer: La Palmyre of the department Charentes Maritimes 17.
Royan, France

Solo Exhibition

InSoon Felch

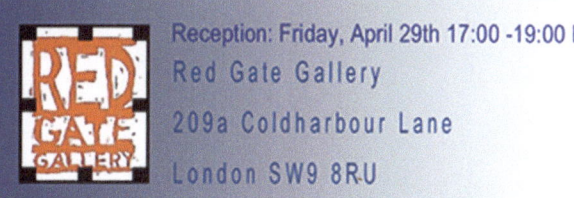

Reception: Friday, April 29th 17:00 -19:00 h
Red Gate Gallery
209a Coldharbour Lane
London SW9 8RU

Defiant of Human Predictability

April 29 - May 5, 2011

Invitational Solo Exhibition, London and Denmark 2011

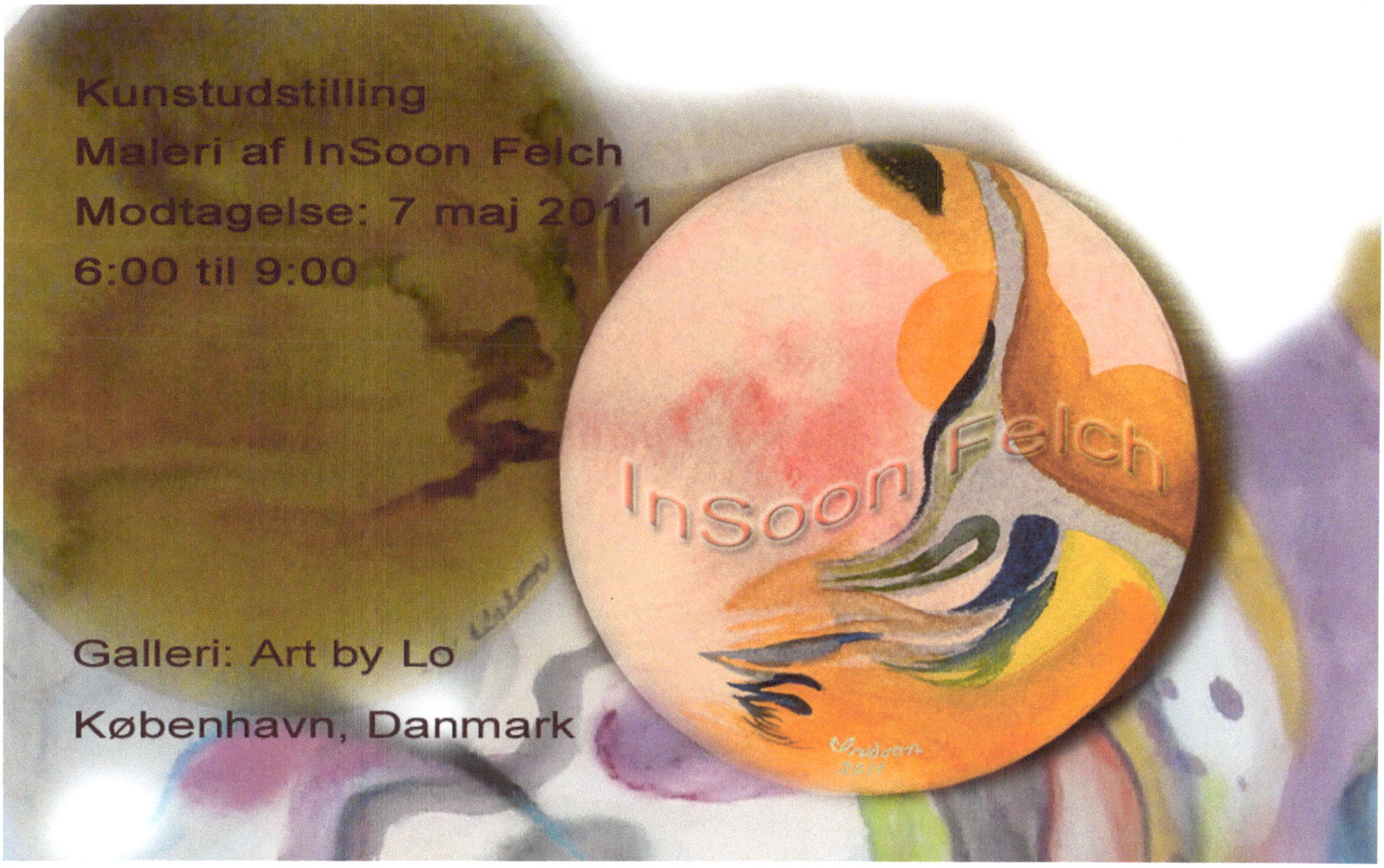

Kunstudstilling
Maleri af InSoon Felch
Modtagelse: 7 maj 2011
6:00 til 9:00

Galleri: Art by Lo

København, Danmark

InSoon Felch

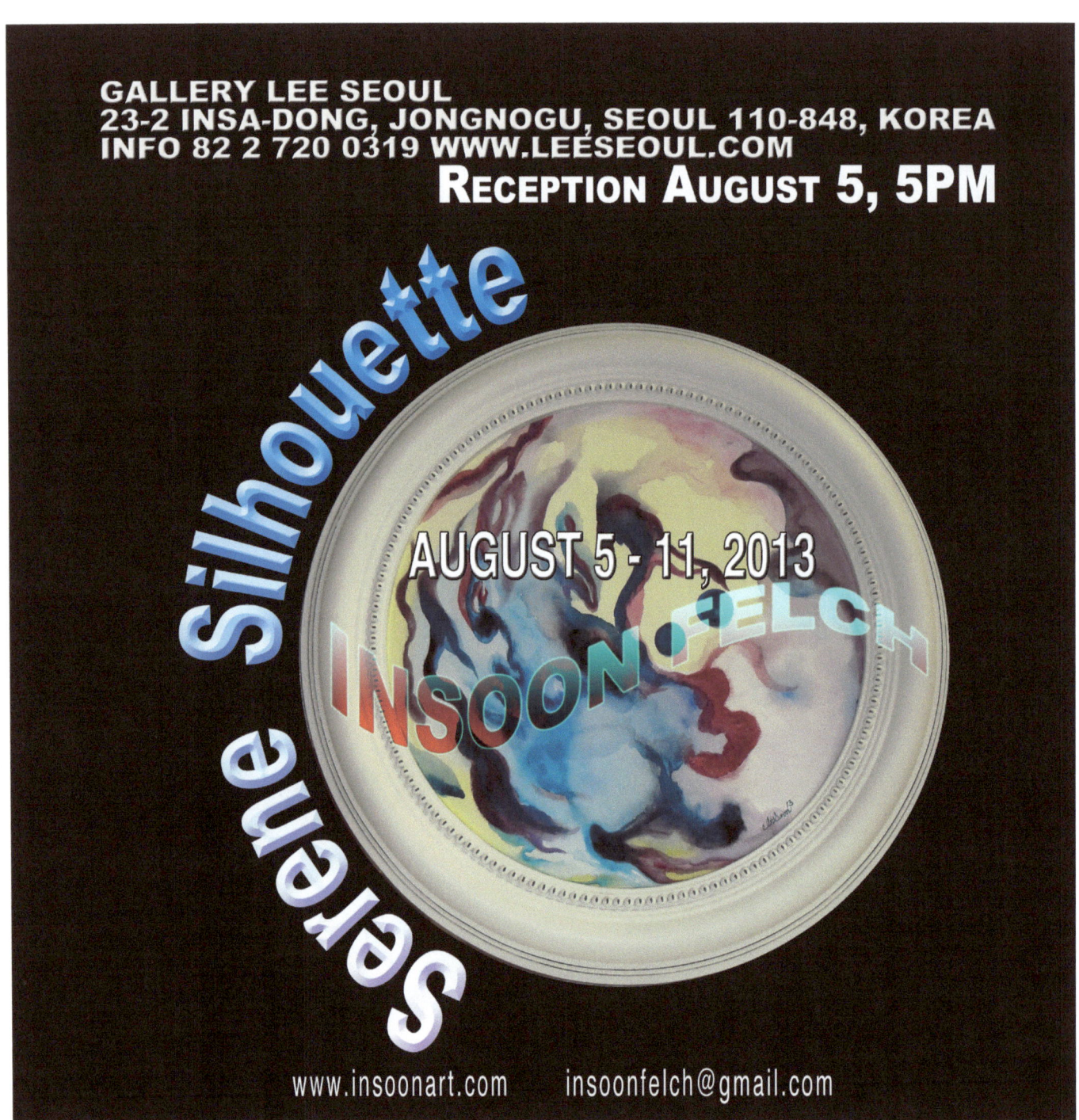

GALLERY LEE SEOUL
23-2 INSA-DONG, JONGNOGU, SEOUL 110-848, KOREA
INFO 82 2 720 0319 WWW.LEESEOUL.COM
RECEPTION AUGUST 5, 5PM

Serene Silhouette

AUGUST 5 - 11, 2013

INSOON FELCH

www.insoonart.com   insoonfelch@gmail.com

Invitational Solo Exhibition, Seoul Insadong 2013

Crossing Boundaries

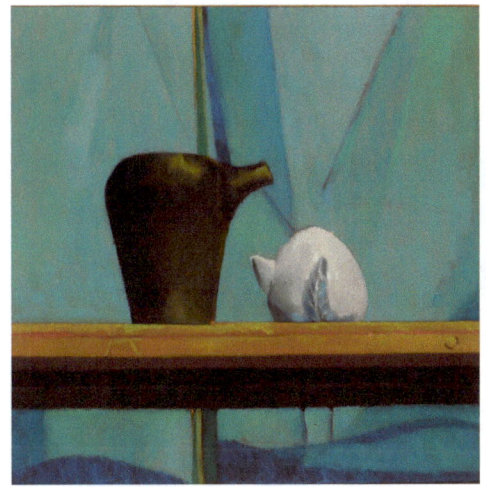
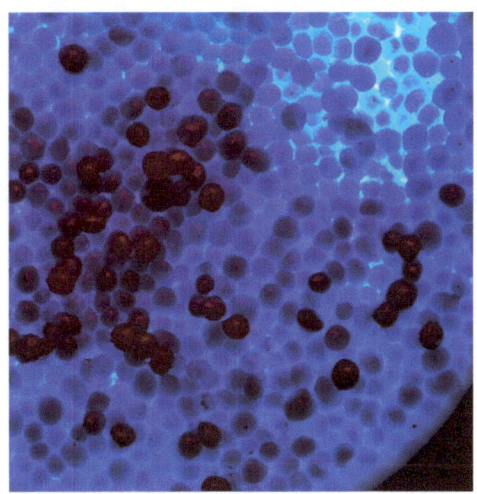
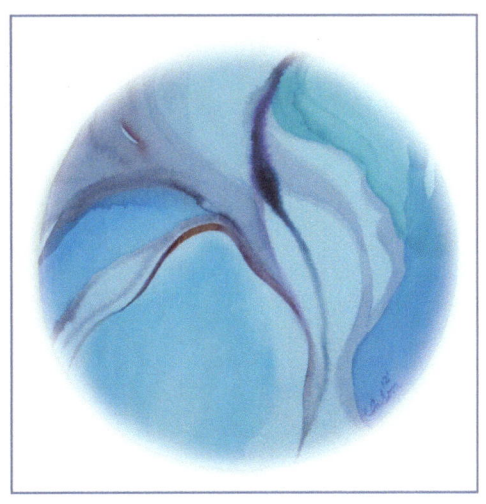
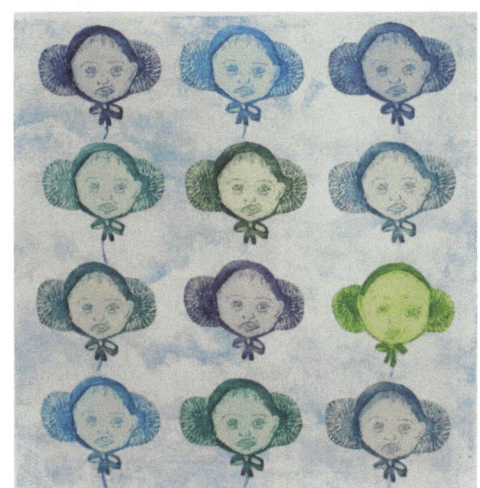

전시명: 경계를 넘어서/**Crossing Boundaries**
한미 여류 화가 초대전

장소: 서울시 종로구 인사동 23-2 리서울 갤러리

기간: 2014년 6월 4일(수) ~6월 10일(화)

리셉션: 2014년 6월 7일 (토요일)

시간: 10: 30 am ~ 6: 30 pm (전시 마지막날은 오전 12시까지 관람 가능합니다.)

문의: 02-720-0319, leeseoul@hanmail.net / www.leeseoul.com

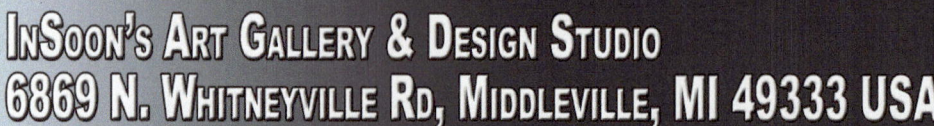

InSoon's Art Gallery & Design Studio
6869 N. Whitneyville Rd, Middleville, MI 49333 USA

MFA in Painting/Sculpture,
BFA in Painting/Computer Graphics,
AA in Art Education
Certified Web Developer/Designer

InSoon Felch

EXHIBITIONS

2014: Invitational Group Exhibition "Women Having Art Therapy" Caledonia, Michigan, USA
2014: 4th Invitational Annual Asian Gala Exhibition sponsored by WMAAA at Goei Center, Grand Rapids, Michigan, USA
2014: Solo Exhibition "Journey from Ashes to Easter" Las Vegas, Nevada, USA
2013: ArtPrize, International Juried Exhibition, "The Beginning and The End" Gerald Ford Presidential Museum, Grand Rapids, Michigan, USA
2013: Solo Exhibition "Serene Silhouette", Lee Seoul Gallery, Insadong, Seoul, Korea
2013: "Castleton on Hudson" Exhibition, Castleton, New York, USA
2013: 3rd Invitational Annual Asian Gala Exhibition sponsored by WMAAA at Goei Center, Grand Rapids, Michigan, USA
2013: "Mutual/ization" Mutuality/Realization: Invitational Worldwide Famous Contemporary Artists, Trio Exhibition, Pera Gallery, Istanbul, Turkey
2013: Solo Exhibition, "To Express and To Live" Claystone Clinic, Grand Rapids, Michigan, USA
2013: Invitational International Exhibition, "Transformation of Consciousness", Van Singel Fine Arts Center, Gainey Gallery, Byron Center, Michigan, USA
2012: ArtPrize, International Juried Exhibition, "Transformation of Consciousness" watercolor & mixed media, Grand Rapids, Michigan, USA
2012: Oregon Society Artists Group Exhibition, Portland, Oregon, USA
2012: Solo Exhibition: Galleria B.R.A.I.N.S. Foundation, Grand Rapids, Michigan
2012: Solo Exhibition: Spatial Conflicts; Integrating Technology and Art, Substation Gallery, Singapore, Singapore
2012: Asian Gala Exhibition, Grand Rapids, Michigan, Keynote Speaker: Governor Rick Snyder, Michigan, USA
2012: Solo Exhibition, Dana Guest House, Bali Island, Indonesia
2011: ArtPrize, International Juried Exhibition, juried by Debbie Knapp, "Aesthetic Empathy" Watercolor, Grand Rapids, Michigan, USA
2011: Solo Exhibition, Art by Lo Gallery, Copenhagen, Denmark
2011: Solo Exhibition, "Defiant of Human Predictability" Red Gate Gallery, London, United Kingdom
2010: Solo Exhibition, B.R.A.I.N.S Foundation, Grand Rapids, Michigan, USA
2010 ArtPrize, International Exhibition, Water building, co-organizer and artist, W.H.A.T. Artists, installation, "Art Out of the Bag" Grand Rapids, Michigan, USA
2009: Solo Exhibition, Phare de la Coubre Gallery, La Tremblade, France
2009 ArtPrize, International Exhibition, Riverview Center, co-organizer and artist, W.H.A.T. Artists, installation, "The ABRAcada-BRA Project: A Show of Support for the Girls!"
Grand Rapids, Michigan, USA
2009: Solo Exhibition, Laura's Heart Studio, Hastings, Michigan, USA
2008: Solo Exhibition "Spatial Elements" Gainey Gallery, VanSingel Fine Arts Center, Byron Center, MI.
2007: Solo Exhibition, Grant Rath's Art Studio, Middleville, Michigan, USA
2005: Solo Exhibition, "Aesthetic Empathy" Keeler lounge, Fountain Street Church, Grand Rapids, Michigan, USA
2003: Solo Exhibition, Thornapple Arts Council, Hastings, Michigan, USA
2002: Solo Exhibition, Pierce Cedar Creek Institute, Hastings, Michigan, USA
2002: Solo Exhibition Thornapple Art Council, Hastings, Michigan, USA
2000: College Art Association Member Group Exhibition, New York, NY, USA
2000: Duet Exhibition, Otherwise Gallery, Lansing, Michigan, USA
2000: MFA Degree Exhibition Rotunda and South Galleries, WMU, Kalamazoo, MI
2000: Annual Student Juried Exhibition, Delton Center, Western Michigan University, Kalamazoo, Michigan, USA
1999: Annual Student Juried Exhibition Delton Center, Western Michigan University, Kalamazoo, Michigan, USA
1999: MFA Group Exhibition, Student Art Gallery, WMU, MI.1998: MFA Group Exhibition, Student Art Gallery, Western Michigan University, Kalamazoo, Michigan, USA
1996: Centralis Senior Project Exhibition sponsored by Honors Office, CMU, Mt. Pleasant, Michigan, USA
1996: Smith Endowment Art Scholarship Recipient Exhibition, Central Michigan University, Michigan, USA
1994: Group Exhibition sponsored by Center for the Arts, Midland, Michigan, USA

www.insoonart.com   insoonfelch@gmail.com

www.ingramcontent.com/pod-product-compliance
Lightning Source LLC
Chambersburg PA
CBHW050417180526
45159CB00005B/2304